Sylvia Pankhurst

Sylvia Pankhurst

A Life in Radical Politics

Mary Davis

Pluto  Press

LONDON • STERLING, VIRGINIA

First published 1999 by Pluto Press
345 Archway Road, London N6 5AA
and 22883 Quicksilver Drive,
Sterling, VA 20166–2012, USA

British Library Cataloguing in Publication Data
A catalogue record for this book is available from the British
Library

ISBN 0 7453 1523 2 hbk

Library of Congress Cataloging-in-Publication Data
Davis, Mary, 1947–
    Sylvia Pankhurst: A Life in Radical Politics / Mary Davis.
        p.   cm.
    Includes bibliographical references and index.
    ISBN 0-7453-1523-2 (hc.)
    1. Pankhurst, E. Sylvia (Estelle Sylvia), 1882–1960.
    2. Feminists–Great Britain Biography. 3. Suffragists–Great
    Britain Biography. I. Title.
    HQ1595.P34038 1999
    305.42'092–dc21
        [B]   9-2(258
                                                                          CIP

Designed and produced for Pluto Press by
Chase Production Services, Chadlington, OX7 3LN
Typeset from disk by Gawcott Typesetting, Buckingham
Printed in the EC by T.J. International, Padstow

FRANCES MARY BUNNAG
(1948–1999)
More than a sister-in-law and better than a sister,
always loved and now always missed.

Contents

Abbreviations

BSP	British Socialist Party
Comintern	Third (Communist) International
CP (BSTI)	Communist Party – British Section of the Third International
CPGB	Communist Party of Great Britain
ELF	East London Federation of the Women's Social and Political Union
ELFS	East London Federation of Suffragettes
IAFA	International African Friends of Abyssinia
IASB	International African Service Bureau
IISH	International Institute of Social History (Amsterdam)
ILP	Independent Labour Party
LRC	Labour Representation Committee
NT&EN	*New Times and Ethiopia News*
NUSEC	National Union of Societies for Equal Citizenship
NUW(C)M	National Unemployed Workers' (Committee) Movement
NUWSS	National Union of Women's Suffrage Societies
PRIB	Peoples' Russia Information Bureau
RILU	Red International of Labour Unions
SDF	Social Democratic Federation
SDP	Social Democratic Party
SLP	Socialist Labour Party
SWSS	South Wales Socialist Society
TUC	Trades Union Congress
UWO	Unemployed Workers' Organisation
VAD	Voluntary Aid Detachment
WEA	Workers' Education Association
WFL	Women's Freedom League
WSF	Workers' Socialist Federation
WSPU	Women's Social and Political Union

Foreword

Mary Davis's *Sylvia Pankhurst: A Life in Radical Politics* is, I feel, of major importance. A work of analysis rather than a biography in the strict sense of the word, it sets the life of my mother, Sylvia Pankhurst, in its historical context. By carefully considering political and other movements, and significant writings of her time, it also throws valuable light on the thinking, prejudices and aspirations of her supporters and opponents. It also reflects on the deepening gulf which gradually separated her from her more conservative mother, Emmeline, and sister, Christabel.

My mother, during a long and active life, was intimately, and well-nigh tirelessly, involved in many different 'causes'. Mary Davis has succeeded in welding these different, and seemingly unrelated, aspects of Sylvia's activities into a comprehensive and very readable narrative. It is centred on three of my mother's principal interests and principles: feminism, socialism and anti-racism. These three driving forces, and particularly her feminism and socialism, explain a fourth of her main concerns: anti-fascism. It was this concern in which she was most passionately engaged in her later years, the years of my childhood and youth.

Sylvia's active opposition to fascism dated back at least to 1919, when she witnessed fascist squads beating up socialists and ordinary citizens in Bologna. Her rejection of fascism in Italy and later in Germany led her, for example, to cross swords on several occasions with Bernard Shaw, who had publicly announced his approval of Mussolini's Corporate State. Replying on 5 December 1932, she declared,

> The Government of Italy ... to all intents and purposes is vested in Mussolini and the small cliques of his satellites in the Fascist Party. Fascism is the regime of a clique maintained by violence and terrorism and by hordes of spies and provocative agents ... The schools are militarised, the little boys of 8 to 14 drilling with wooden rifles and the boys over 14 with real rifles

... The boys are taught that their aim in life should be to be a soldier; the girls to marry early, have their cradles full and bear soldiers to extend the dominions of Italy.

All the best positions are reserved for members of the Fascist Party ... The women fascists are subordinated to the men ... and the woman secretary takes her orders not from their own members but from the man secretary of the corresponding male fascist unit. The press is gagged, censored and dictated to, and only the fascist press is permitted.

Culturally speaking, fascism is reactionary and repressive and this has been painfully discovered by authors who had no desire to take part in politics, again and again.

The Corporate State ... is simply a euphemistic phrase to indicate that the workers are to remain content in the station of life in which they are born; that their betters are to do the thinking and that they must carry out the toil of the community, as the hands and feet of the human body do the will of the directing brain, without presuming either to express an opinion, or to cherish a desire or an aspiration of their own.

She saw in fascism, as the above passage shows, the negation not only of the rights of the citizen, but also, more specifically, the suppression of women's and workers' rights.

Sylvia's anti-racism (and, by extension, her opposition to colonialism), which has been ignored by most earlier writers on her life and activities, is particularly well documented by Mary Davis. It helps to explain the last phase of my mother's life. It was then that she espoused the cause of Ethiopia, at that time, other than Liberia, the only independent state on the African continent. As an anti-fascist, she watched Mussolini's plans to invade with foreboding, and subsequently founded a newspaper in its defence. Italy, as she saw it, was the first victim of Mussolini's fascism; Ethiopia the second.

Though later a no less committed supporter of the Republican side during the Spanish civil war – and of other 'victim nations' assailed by the fascist powers – Sylvia refused to abandon her concern for the far-off African country. When asked to do so by the Labour leader, Stafford Cripps, who believed British workers were more interested in their fellow Europeans in nearby Spain, she refused, replying, on 26 August 1936, 'With regard to Ethiopia and Spain, it seems to me that the more we press both questions home, the more we show what fascism is really doing in the world.'

By concentrating on the three fields of feminism, socialism and anti-racism, Mary Davis has succeeded in placing my mother's life in a useful perspective, which may help the reader to unravel the dynamic of Sylvia's contribution to her times.

Richard Pankhurst
Addis Ababa, 1999

Biographical Note and Political Background

1882   Estelle Sylvia Pankhurst, born in Old Trafford, Manchester, second child of Richard (d.1898) and Emmeline (d.1928). One older sister, Christabel, (1880–1958); two younger brothers, Frank (died aged 4 in 1888) and Harry (died aged 21 in 1910); one younger sister, Adela (1885–1961).

1893   Independent Labour Party (ILP) formed; both parents join and are on friendly terms with many of its leaders, including James Keir Hardie.

1897   National Union of Women's Suffrage Societies (NUWSS) formed.

1900   Sylvia wins scholarship to study design at Manchester School of Art.
        Labour Representation Committee (LRC) formed.

1903   Women's Social and Political Union (WSPU) founded by Emmeline Pankhurst. Sylvia designs its logo.

1904   After a two-year stay in Venice to study art, Sylvia moves to London where she enrols as a student at the Royal College of Art. She is already a convinced socialist and maintains a close friendship with Keir Hardie until his death in 1915.

1906   Liberal election victory.
        The WSPU moves its headquarters to London. Emmeline and Frederick Pethick-Lawrence become closely involved in the organisation and with their financial support, the WSPU grows rapidly. Sylvia is involved in its activities although she is critical of its stance on many issues, especially its attitude to the labour movement.
        Sylvia sent to Holloway Prison for 'obstructive and abusive language'.

1907   The WSPU severs its connection with the ILP and in addition abandons its democratic constitution. This

	leads Edith How Martyn, Teresa Billington Greig and Charlotte Despard to form a breakaway organisation, the Women's Freedom League.
1908	Asquith replaces Campbell-Bannerman as Liberal Prime Minister and declares his opposition to women's suffrage. Beginning of 'militant' campaign.
1909	WSPU launches its campaign of direct action.
	Sylvia visits the working-class districts of the north of England and Scotland to paint and write about the conditions of women workers in the mining, fishing, pottery and chain-making industries.
	Suffragette prisoners go on hunger strike. Forcible feeding introduced.
1910	Suffrage measure in the form of a Conciliation Bill introduced but not passed. Sylvia goes on speaking tour of USA.
	Beginning of the 'great unrest' – massive strike wave organised by syndicalists.
1911	Sylvia goes on speaking tour of USA.
1912	Emmeline and Frederick Pethick-Lawrence expelled from the WSPU.
	WSPU militancy takes a more violent form. Christabel directs operations from her exile in Paris. Sylvia moves to the East End and organises suffrage work there.
	George Lansbury stands as a women's suffrage candidate in the East End constituency of Bow and Bromley.
	Manhood Suffrage Bill introduced.
	Labour-suffrage alliance formed (Labour Party and NUWSS).
1914	Sylvia expelled from the WSPU. The East London Federation of Suffragettes (ELFS) launched as an independent organisation with its weekly paper, the *Woman's Dreadnought*.
1914	August: Britain enters the First World War.
	Most women's suffrage organisations, except ELFS, support the war effort.
	WSPU paper, *Votes for Women*, is renamed *Britannia*.
1915	ELFS launches its campaign for equal pay for women and an end to 'sweating'.
1916	Asquith declares his intention of introducing a suffrage bill (to include women) after the war.
	ELFS declares in favour of 'human suffrage'.

	ELFS renamed Workers' Suffrage Federation.
1917	Russian revolution.
	Woman's Dreadnought renamed the *Workers' Dreadnought.*
1918	Women over 30 enfranchised.
	Bus and tube women workers strike for equal pay.
	Sylvia establishes Peoples' Russia Information Bureau (PRIB).
	'Hands Off Russia' campaign launched.
	Workers' Suffrage Federation renamed Workers' Socialist Federation (WSF).
1919	Third Communist International formed – WSF applies for affiliation.
	Sylvia travels to Continental Europe, meeting leading lefts and 'ultras'.
	Meeting of representatives of WSF, British Socialist Party, South Wales Socialist Society and Socialist Labour Party – provisional committee established, from which WSF withdraw in June 1920.
1920	London dockers refuse to load the 'Jolly George'.
	Lenin's 21 principles.
	Councils of Action formed to combat threat of British invasion of Soviet Russia. Sylvia in Moscow for Second Congress of the Third International.
	Communist Party – British Section of the Third International (CP (BSTI)) launched in Manchester (ex-WSF).
	Sylvia arrested on charges of sedition.
	Communist Unity Convention.
1921	Leeds Unity Convention – Communist Party of Great Britain (CPGB) established, including the CP (BSTI).
	Sylvia expelled from CPGB.
1922	Mussolini's March on Rome; Sylvia begins her anti-fascist work.
1923	French troops occupy the Ruhr.
	Claude McKay employed as a journalist on *Workers' Dreadnought.*
1924	First Labour government (minority).
	Workers' Dreadnought ceases publication.
1926	Publication of *India and the Earthly Paradise.*
1927	Birth of Richard Pankhurst.
1930	Publication of *Save the Mothers.*

1932	Sylvia forms Women's International Matteotti Committee.
1934	Sylvia is Treasurer of International Women's Committee Against War and Fascism.
1935	Italian invasion of Ethiopia. Sylvia publishes first edition of *New Times and Ethiopia News (NT&EN)*.
1936	Spanish Civil War. Haile Selassie's appeal to the League of Nations.
1937	International Africa Service Bureau founded: Sylvia is a member of Committee of Associates.
1939	*NT&EN* banned in Sierre Leone. Second World War – Sylvia is secretary of Women's War Emergency Council.
1940	Italy declares war on Britain: BBC play Ethiopian national anthem.
1941	Allied liberation of Ethiopia: much of the country under British occupation. Ethiopia forced to sign the First (1942) and Second (1944) Anglo-Ethiopian Agreements.
1944	Sylvia's first visit to Ethiopia.
1945	Pan African Congress, Manchester.
1945–6	Protest meetings and rallies in London against British policy in Ethiopia.
1948	Sylvia joins Labour Party.
1954	Britain withdraws from 'Reserved Areas'; *NT&EN* ceases publication.
1956	Sylvia goes to live in Ethiopia.
1960	Sylvia Pankhurst dies, aged 78.

Introduction

It is only just over 70 years since women have had full suffrage in Britain. The vote for women came in two stages: 1918, when women over 30 with a small property qualification were enfranchised; and 1928, which 'swept away the absurd restrictions'[1] of the previous act. There are many books which deal with the long campaign for women's suffrage[2] – this is not one of them. Rather it is an attempt to analyse the relationship between the two most powerful movements for social change at the turn of the century, the women's movement and the labour movement.

The alliance (such as it was) between the two movements was problematic. Underlying it was, and still is, the vexed question of the relationship between class and gender, and between feminism and socialism. It was this question above all others which led to a major and irreversible split within one of the most important of the women's suffrage organisations, the Women's Social and Political Union (WSPU: the suffragettes). This split mirrored the ideological rift within the Pankhurst family, the founders and prime movers of the WSPU. Sylvia Pankhurst was expelled from the organisation by her mother, Emmeline, and her elder sister, Christabel, because she persisted in pursuing an alliance with the labour movement. Sylvia was not the only or the first active feminist to view the liberation of women to be indissolubly connected to the wider struggle to end class exploitation. However, because the women's movement and the labour movement exercised such a powerful influence in the immediate pre- and post-First World War years, her work in this period (and beyond) in attempting to forge the link between the two issues is particularly important and repays serious study.

This book does not pretend to be a biography of Sylvia Pankhurst,[3] although a sympathetic, non-hagiographical, account of her life remains to be written.[4] She has never received the attention she deserves by historians of the women's movement or the labour movement. Taking their cue from the WSPU leadership, Sylvia's contribution to winning the vote has been underestimated and her work as a revolutionary socialist has often been belittled or relegated to a footnote. In attempting to redress this imbalance my purpose is not to reify Sylvia and her contribution to changing the lot of women or the working class, but rather to re-examine her work in the context of women's and labour politics in order to shed further light on the still current complexites of the relationship between socialism and feminism. Any serious student of the labour movement, feminist or not, needs to pay as much attention to Sylvia as has been given to her male contemporaries like George Lansbury or Keir Hardie. By the same token, our knowledge of the women's suffrage movement has suffered from an undue emphasis on the suffragettes[5] (the Women's Social and Political Union) alone. This tendency has been remedied in recent years by some pioneering research on the activities of working-class women in the north of England.[6] The work of Sylvia Pankhurst in London's East End sheds light on the contribution made by countless unsung working-class women who were as dedicated to the women's suffrage campaign as their more publicity-conscious middle-class sisters.

However, this is not the whole story. Apart from the fact that during her long and active life Sylvia founded and edited four newspapers, wrote and published 22 books and pamphlets (not to mention literally countless articles); she was also a founder and tireless activist in a variety of women's, labour movement and international solidarity organisations. Her most recent biographer, Barbara Winslow,[7] has filled a well-researched and scholarly volume chronicling Sylvia's activities up to 1924. Given that she remained active until her death in 1960, it would take another two volumes at least to complete the task. None the less, this book attempts to explore her activities in the post-suffrage period in respect of two other areas in which she made a pioneering contribution: revolutionary communist politics, and anti-racism and anti-fascism. In relation to the former, her activity was short lived, especially in comparison with her over 30 year involvement in anti-fascism, anti-racism and the cause of Ethiopia – the country which became her home for the last four years of her life and in which she was buried.

The research for and the writing of this book has provided many surprises, some of which have altered my views of a historical period I thought I knew well. It has also resulted in a surprise discovery; namely the papers of Nellie Cressall, an East-Ender active in the East London Federation of Suffragettes

(ELFS) from the outset, followed by close involvement in Poplar politics. I am indebted to Mick Mears for introducing me to the 'guardians' of Nellie Cressall's papers, namely her grandaughters, Linda Harris, Jenny Maynard and Sylvia Mears. Whilst I have made only very limited use of the papers here, they will form the basis of a forthcoming book about Nellie Cressall, one of the many working-class women who made a significant contribution to suffrage and labour history but whose story has never been told.

In addition, this study, especially of the suffrage campaign and Sylvia's role in it, raises many tactical and strategic issues which face feminist, anti-racist and socialist activists today. It poses questions about single-issue politics, the nature of alliances and, in particular, in the case of women's suffrage (and, indeed, many other 'women's issues' of today), the relationship between gender and class. Does a non-class perspective alter the nature of the issue and, as a consequence, the manner in which the campaign around it is conducted? How broad should alliances be, and should tactics be modified in order to win and keep allies? Are alliances necessary at all – is the cause best served by a small, dedicated group prepared to make heroic sacrifices? Should the caution of the many hold back the impatience of the few? Do the ends justify the means – is any tactic valid provided the goal is finally achieved? Is the inherently progressive nature of the cause altered, or even lost sight of, if its class content is not recognised from the outset?

Such questions and many like them will be familiar to anyone who has been active in the labour, the women's or the anti-racist movements. They surface in the period covered by the book, and certainly were uppermost in Sylvia Pankhurst's work. She was a great campaigner, and whilst she did not nor could not iron out all the difficulties, she had a shrewd sense of how to build a movement. Much could be learned from her.

It is not altogether surprising, though none the less infuriating, that there is no permanent memorial to Sylvia Pankhurst, especially given that the British state has chosen to honour Emmeline and Christabel, with a statue for the former and a plaque for the latter, both outside the House of Commons. I believe that I am not alone in taking the view that Sylvia's strategy, based as it was on an alliance between class and gender, did far more to win the vote for all women than the more elitist and ultimately diversionary politics of her mother and elder sister. Sylvia would not have liked a memorial, but as a symbol of the unsung heroism of thousands of working-class women who fought for the franchise and for socialism, some kind of recognition in the form of a statue of Sylvia Pankhurst is not only long overdue, but would, at long last, help correct the historical record.

I am grateful to the specialist libraries (all mentioned in the bibliography) for the use of archive and other primary source material. I am particularly grateful to Richard Pankhurst (Sylvia's son) for taking the trouble to answer my written questions, to meet me and to read the manuscript, and above all, for writing the foreword. Anne Beech of Pluto Press has been kind, very patient and wise throughout: she too has my thanks.

Mary Davis
1999

1

Separate Spheres – the Labour Movement and the Women's Suffrage Movement

The last two decades of the nineteenth century witnessed a momentous change in British politics. The extension of the franchise in 1884 to almost all adult males, together with the expansion of literacy, is variously described by historians and contemporaries as inaugurating 'the era of the masses', 'the age of democracy'. This was not a purely British phenomenon. Under pressure from an increasingly strong socialist movement, most European countries underwent similar democratising changes in these decades. Reflecting, and to an extent directing, the spirit of the age, the women's suffrage movement and the labour movement in Britain developed a mass appeal in this period. Neither movement was new, but both, for different reasons, began to appeal on gender lines to a wider working-class audience. However, the winds of change did not extend to the female of half of Britain's population, who remained unenfranchised and excluded from public life. The extent to which this stunted democracy was seen as a solely women's issue determined not only the success of winning the demand for women's franchise, but also the degree to which the women's movement and the labour movement could work together.

However, the singular peculiarity of the upsurge of these late ninetenth-century mass movements of protest is that they remained bound, unlike those of the first half of the century, in their separate spheres.[1] With notable exceptions, the labour movement paid little attention to the demands of women, and, apart from the radical suffragists in textile areas of the north of England, the predominant middle-class voice within the women's movement paid little attention to the demands of the labour movement. It was only at the edges of the two movements that any convergence occurred. Within the women's movement, Sylvia Pankhurst was one of the small band of fem-

inists who advocated such a course. Within the labour movement, men like Keir Hardie and George Lansbury also worked
against the predominant patriarchal tide. All were class-conscious socialists, although as we shall see, socialism did not
axiomatically embrace women's suffrage, much less feminism,
in these years.

The Labour Movement

The fortunes of the long established British labour movement
underwent a considerable revival in the late 1880s. New socialist organisations like the Social Democratic Federation (SDF)
and the Independent Labour Party (ILP) spearheaded the political break with lib-labism,[2] whilst the stranglehold of the
'aristocracy of labour' in the trade unions was challenged by the
rapid (initially at least) recruitment of unskilled and semi-skilled
workers. By 1900, the two wings of the labour movement had
begun a process of fusion that was to result in the formation of
Labour Party.

Trade Unions

The socialist revival of the 1880s, pre-dating the revival of the
women's movement by over a decade, was deeply imbued with
the patriarchal attitudes and sexist prejudices of Victorian
England. For 30 years or so, since the 1850s, the trade union
movement had been a predominantly male preserve with an all-
male leadership. The only unions with women members were
the textile unions. Indeed, the prime concern of most male
trade unions was to restrict women's labour and preserve the
traditional position of women as homemakers, wives and
mothers. Women workers, in the third quarter of the nineteenth century, had suffered a great defeat. The only trade in
which they still remained organised in any numbers was that of
weaving. The aim of trade unionism, according to Henry
Broadhurst, secretary of the TUC, speaking in 1875, was 'to
bring about a condition ... where wives and daughters would be
in their proper sphere at home, instead of being dragged into
competition for livelihood against the great and strong men of
the world'.[3] From this kind of thinking sprang the widespread
acceptance of the notion of the 'family wage' to be won by the
male breadwinner. Hence not only was unequal pay accepted as

a norm, but women's work was only tolerated if not threatening to men. In any case, it was seen as a mark of shame if a man permitted his wife to work, hence the widespread practice, hardly contested by the unions until the twentieth century, of barring married women from employment altogether. Such attitudes and practices help to explain women's increasing job segregation and the fact that so much female labour was literally hidden. It is not surprising, therefore, that the unions of this period demonstrated a studied indifference, if not downright hostility, to women workers. Any attempts to organise women in this period came from outside the labour movement, often through the work of philanthropic women. So, although the development of trade unions among unskilled workers from the late 1880s offered some hope for women, in practice these deeply entrenched patriarchal attitudes remained a massive barrier. Despite the spectacular increase in trade union membership, especially after 1910, the fact remains that by 1914, 90 per cent of all trade unionists were men and over 90 per cent of women remained unorganised. Half of the 10 per cent of organised women were members of one or other of the textile unions and the remainder were members of the new unions formed for shop workers, clerical workers and teachers. All of these trades and occupations were predominantly female.

Although the syndicalist-inspired 'great unrest' of 1910–14 challenged the complacency of the established trade union leadership, it did little to confront deeply entrenched patriarchal attitudes and practices. This was all the more surprising given that the massive strike wave of these years coincided with the most active phase of the women's suffrage campaign. Whilst the strategy and tactics of the main women's suffrage organisation, in these years,[4] the Women's Social and Political Union (WSPU), may be offered as a partial explanation for this, it is by no means the main reason for syndicalism's studied indifference, and in some cases downright hostility, to the women's cause. Syndicalism was a rank-and-file revolt against what was perceived as the incorporation of labour and trade union leaders into the capitalist system at a time when the employers' offensive, especially in the staple industries, was making a determined effort to maintain the rate of profit by driving down the rate of wages. Syndicalists aimed to regain workers' control over workplace wages and conditions by utilising direct action, in the form of the mass strike and rapid trade union all-grades recruitment. At a deeper level it was inspired by

a theoretical vision, extant in various forms in many industri-
alised countries, of jettisoning the entire capitalist system by
establishing workers' control of industry. In this regard its
appeal was inevitably limited to the big industrial battalions
from which women were largely excluded. A strike in a pickle
factory, a laundry or an office could not be equated, in syndicalist terms, with a strike in an industry at the heart of the
productive process like mining or engineering. But in any case,
syndicalism's total focus on workplace struggles and hostility to
the parliamentary process meant an explicit rejection of wider
political issues, like the franchise for women. Hence it was
perhaps not surprising that *The Syndicalist*[5] barely mentioned
the suffrage campaign other than to condemn the violent
tactics of the WSPU and the foolhardiness of desiring the vote
for women. The paper published 'An open letter to the WSPU',[6]
which started by stating that since syndicalists do not attach
any importance to the vote, 'the material objects of your agitation, therefore, do not recommend themselves to us'. It went on
to offer patronising advice to 'Mesdames of the Women's Social
and Political Union' who, it claimed, were part of an organisation which 'is one of the richest in the world'. Notwithstanding
this, the anonymous author of the article argued that the WSPU
had 'failed to make any lasting impression or gain any permanent good-will among the millions of exploited women workers
in this country'. Such criticism might have been more credible
if the journal had at least acknowledged the fact that whilst
working-class women were absent from the ranks of the WSPU,
they were not absent from the campaign for women's suffrage.
There was no mention of the painstaking efforts of women
factory workers in the northern textile districts, nor of the
solidly working-class campaign in the East End of London led
by Sylvia.[7] Perhaps the lack of honesty in reflecting the genuine
and widespread demand for the vote by women of all classes is
explained by a deeper misogynism which was revealed in an
article entitled 'In criticism of Christabel'. This was a review of
Christabel Pankhurst's frankly ludicrous book, *The Great
Scourge*.[8] 'Homo', the author of the article, judged the entire
women's movement on the basis of what he classed as 'the side-
tracking, by a few sex-mad spinsters ... in a direction of a revolt
against the male sex'. From this he concluded:

> I am sorry to have to acknowlege that not a little truth was
> contained in the predictions of those Anti-Suffragists of some

years ago who decreed the women's revolt as a revolt against all those 'fine institutions of marriage and motherhood upon which our civilisation is built'.[9]

Thus it was that although the great forward movement of labour in the four years prior to the First World War accomplished much in inspiring a new form of militant rank-and-file trade unionism, it did little to challenge the deeply entrenched patriarchal attitiudes which perpetuated women's second-class status in society and in the workplace. As a purely workplace reflection of the aspirations of working-class activists, syndicalism was perhaps ill equipped to embrace the wider ideological battle. This, it could be argued, was the function of socialist political parties. Since the decline of the Chartist movement in the early 1850s, there had been no independent working-class political organisation. This 30 year deficit was remedied in the 1880s and 1890s with the formation of the SDF and the ILP.

The Social Democratic Federation

Of the two political organisations formed in the last two decades of the nineteenth century, the SDF (1884) and the ILP (1893), it was the latter which offered more hope for women, despite the fact that the SDF was avowedly Marxist and therefore supposedly more 'advanced'. E. Belfort Bax, a leading member of the SDF and of its successors (the Social Democratic Party (SDP), 1909, and the British Socialist Party (BSP), 1911)[10] and close associate of William Morris,[11] was not only opposed to women's suffrage but was deeply misogynistic. At the height of the suffrage agitation he published *The Fraud of Feminism* (1913), a truly amazing diatribe against the very notion of women's equality. Were it not for the fact that Belfort Bax was known as a leading Marxist intellectual (dubbed by William Morris as 'the philosopher of the movement'), this book might be dismissed along with the countless other anti-suffrage broadsides emanating from the threatened male establishment. But Belfort Bax in other respects was not an establishment figure, and although his views might be considered as extreme even by the standards of the day, they were not challenged ideologically within the Marxist left in Britain, despite the fact that in Continental European Marxist circles they would have been considered primaeval. Belfort Bax published his first anti-feminist tract in 1908 (*The Legal Subjugation of Men*), the very year in which, responding to the call from women of the Second International, the first Women's Day (later International Women's Day) demonstration was held in New York. Engels had, two decades earlier, published his *Origins of the Family Private Property and the State* (1884) and Bebel, the leading German socialist, had published his *Women and Socialism* in 1878. Both books analysed the origins of women's oppression and stoutly defended women's rights and equality from a Marxist standpoint. Whether Belfort Bax was aware or not of these developments, it is quite clear that his work on the question of women showed not a single sign of a Marxist analysis. It is based on the commonly understood presumption of 'the average woman being intellectually below the voting standard, and the average man as not'.[12] This, said Belfort Bax, was due to her smaller brain size, which in turn had been determined by the physiological and anatomical difference between the two sexes based on fact that 'man *has* a sex, woman *is* sex'. This resulted in (according to Belfort Bax) women's prime function as procreators and men's function in developing the technological, moral and intellectual progress of society. As a consequence, 'the brain of the man grew with the progress of civilization, whereas that of the woman remains nearly stationary'.[13] Hence Belfort Bax not only rejected the demand for women's suffrage, but opposed all demands for 'so-called rights' which emerged from the late eighteenth century onwards. On this basis he lamented the progress women had made throughout the nineteenth century and viewed the whole panoply of 'unilateral sex legislation' on such matters as divorce, education, and municipal voting rights as having led to a situation 'by which the whole power of the state is practically at the disposal of women to coerce and oppress men'.[14] Thus, in an astounding rejection of the very limited gains women had made, Belfort Bax appeared seriously to believe that women were now the oppressors.

Belfort Bax's views have been discussed because, whilst not 'typical' of labour movement thinking, they represent – albeit in a most extreme form – a strand of antipathy to women's rights which confirmed the male domination of the movement and made it unwelcoming for women. Indeed, even a committed SDF activist like Dora Montefiore (later a foundation member of the Communist Party), resigned from the executive committee of the Federation in 1905 because she could not tolerate its attitude to women members. She had established a women's committee, but found that it was valued for its 'labours in providing the refreshments served'.[15] Belfort Bax did not cover his antipathy to women by the more usual device of writing off feminism as the concern of middle-class 'ladies' and hence a diversion from the class struggle. It would have been difficult even for him to sustain such an argument in the early twentieth century when it was clear that working-class women were deeply involved in the battle for the vote, in Britain and most other countries besides. Indeed it is only this conviction of women's inferiority that can explain why the SDF, SDP and BSP remained steadfastly hostile to women's suffrage as a point of principle, even at a time when other organisations of the labour movement were beginning to change their stance. Harry Quelch of the SDF (SDP and BSP) could be relied upon to oppose the demand for women's suffrage in whatever forum it was proposed.

In 1911, the SDP, in an important move to unify the left, had taken the initiative in establishing a new organisation, the British Socialist Party (its first conference was held in 1912). This development occurred at the height of the 'great unrest' – a period of unparalleled industrial militancy. Unlike its predecessors, the BSP actively sought, according to its First Annual Report, 'the closest possible co-operation with trade union organisations, and the advocacy of industrial unity of all workers'. This was an important and non-sectarian departure in view of the fact that the party remained critical of the syndicalist leadership of the industrial struggle. It was, in addition, a sharp contrast to the SDF's previously hostile attitude to trade unions. But political maturity on this important issue was not. parallelled by a change of attitude to the movement for women's suffrage which was, during the same period (1910–14) able to mobilise countless thousands of women into active campaigning. The columns of *Justice*, the weekly paper of the BSP (the title having been retained from the early days of the SDF), were full of reports and analyses of the industrial struggle, including information about BSP branches' active campaigning. There is, however, very little information on the women's suffrage campaign, other than of a critical nature. The beginnings of a debate on the suffrage question were opened in 1912 with the publication of an article by Leonard Hall in which he draws a parallel between the industrial struggle and the women's struggle. Whilst welcoming BSP support for the former, he notes with disapproval that the party is silent on the latter and goes on to deplore the trials and imprisonment of suffrage activists. (The article was written at the time of the much publicised trial of Mrs Pankhurst and her two close associates, Emmeline and Frederick

Pethick-Lawrence.) The BSP line is revealed in an editorial note published at the end of Hall's piece. In it, the editors explain that Hall's article was published because it gives a good defence of the militant suffragettes, but 'for ourselves we disclaim all sympathy with their tactics', arguing that it is incorrect to draw a parallel with their actions and that of strike action by industrial workers. Although serving terms of imprisonment the women 'have taken advantage of their sex to take action which would be impossible for men'.[16] In an article (presumably solicited) written the following week, F. J. Gould went much further. He declared that he was 'not prepared to give assistance to a non-socialist body like the Women's Social and Political Union, or to throw away any enthusiasm on people like the Pethick-Lawrences who place the women's suffrage above the vital economic question'. Gould anyway disliked women 'rioting' and saw 'a far better quality in the angry outbreaks of men who were moved by thoughts of their families than in the angry outbursts of women who could scarcely be regarded as moved by family sympathies'.[17] Only two other letters were published in this 'debate', both from men. Two letters were received from women, but the editor declined to publish them on the grounds that 'their claim to speak for women generally would ... be contested by other women in the movement'.[18] Instead Belfort Bax was allowed to hold forth, possibly on the assumption that no one would contest his claim to speak for everyone! His views remained as misogynistic as ever. He saw no parallel between the suffrage and industrial struggles, but opposed the former on the grounds that it was another step on the road to 'sex domination' by women. Needless to say, he had no sympathy for suffrage prisoners, in fact he thought they were treated too leniently. Further debate on the issue was curtailed with the announcement that a series of special articles had been commissioned explaining the BSP's view on women's suffrage. Five articles appeared between the end of July and the end of August 1912 entitled 'Social democracy and votes for women'. The BSP held the WSPU's campaign of violence and arson responsible for the failure of the Reform Bill introduced in 1912 by Asquith. This was essentially a manhood suffrage bill and as such was welcomed by the BSP, although all sections of the women's movement and, by now, almost all strands of the labour movement were united in condemning the government's refusal to include women's suffrage in its proposals. (In 1913 the Speaker of the House of Commons expressly ruled out the possibility of any amendment along such lines.) Clearly the BSP was out on a limb, but justified its support for the government's Bill by concentrating its attack on the questionable tactics employed by the militant suffragettes. However, the tone and the content of the attack revealed a deeply unsympathetic attitude to the women's suffrage movement generally. In condemning the violent tactics used by some women, the BSP rejected the view that more had been achieved in the past 'five years to advance the cause of women than forty years of peaceful campaigning'; rather their 'antics' had simply called 'attention to a grievance which only an insignificant minority regard as grievance at all'.[19] These women 'hooligans' and 'mad creatures' (*Justice's* terms) were middle class and cared little for adult suffrage, which was 'of all things the most odious and hateful to them. Far better that no women should have the vote than all women should be enfranchised.'[20] This was a reference to the fact that the WSPU demand for the vote 'on the same terms as men' had implied a vote based on a property qualification. However, as the BSP well knew, the suffragette line was in favour of dropping the property qualification if it was dropped for men also. In other words, there was no opposition to full adult suffrage – the real difference was over the question of manhood suffrage. The WSPU had declared its position unequivocally in 1912: 'We shall refuse to be content with anything less than a Government measure to give equal franchise rights to men and women.'[21] The BSP was reduced to the somewhat feeble line of suggesting that if the government's manhood suffrage bill was passed, the WSPU should have supported the call for a referendum on women's suffrage. The final article, in language and essence smacking of Belfort Bax, asserted that the suffragettes were not even in favour of the vote and deliberately sabotaged the movement: 'These women, excitable, hysterical, vain and histrionic, carried away with finding themselves so much in the public eye, realised that the granting of votes to women would deprive them of their occupation.'[22]

As subsequent chapters show, there is much to be questioned in the tactics and ideology of the WSPU leadership. (Sylvia herself was highly critical.) However, there was nothing in these five major articles to distinguish between the issue of women's suffrage itself and the means used to gain it. Neither is there any recognition of the fact that other women's organisations with a substantial working-class following and using the more traditional methods of mass mobilisation, were also opposed to any reform of the franchise which omitted women. Clearly, despite the positive and unifying role it was attempting to play on the industrial front, the BSP had not yet rid itself of the chauvinism and sectarianism of its SDF past on the issue of women's franchise.

The Independent Labour Party

The ILP, founded in Bradford in 1893, had an active working-class women's membership from its inception, rooted as it was in the textile districts of north west England. Two leading supporters of women's suffrage, Isabella Ford and Sylvia's mother, Emmeline, were elected to the national leadership and one of its founding members, Keir Hardie, was a strong supporter of votes for women. None the less, in its early years the party paid little or no attention to this question. It was only at the 1902 conference that the policy was adopted in a motion proposed by Mrs Pankhurst, although at the same conference, a motion was also passed calling for adult suffrage. By 1904, however, the ILP had declared itself unreservedly in favour of a women's suffrage bill and re-affirmed this position at each subsequent annual conference. From then on the ILP can be regarded as the most steadfast champion of the women's cause and was the main vehicle for campaigning for a change of attitude within the labour movement as a whole. Keir Hardie himself must take much of the credit for this. His support for feminism, nurtured by his friendship with Sylvia, and allied to his socialism, led him to argue consistently that women's suffrage was an issue of principle for the labour movement. This commitment, together with his standing in the labour movement, enabled him to navigate a difficult course through the countervailing opposition which at various times used the argument of adult suffrage, distaste for WSPU tactics and the perceived middle-class nature of the women's movement as reasons to frustrate support for the cause.

In an attempt to disprove the commonly stated view that the main beneficiaries of the current women's suffrage bill would be middle-class 'ladies', Hardie conducted an ILP survey in 1905.[23] This, together with similar surveys completed by Selina Cooper (Nelson) and others by members of the Co-operative Women's Guild, attempted to prove that if the existing household and lodger franchise (the basis of male suffrage since 1884) was extended to women (the basis of the suffrage demand), 80 per cent of the women enfranchised would be working-class.[24] This exercise must be seen as part of the attempt to refute the argument (which still surfaces today) that the women's struggle was a diversion from class politics. It was aimed as much at winning hearts and minds in the ILP itself, which had taken a brave and minority stance within the labour movement. Indeed, by 1907 it was evident that there was some doubt within the ILP as to the wisdom of the policy. Certainly the WSPU leadership's break with the ILP and Labour Party in 1907 did not help to allay misgivings (see Chapter 2). The ILP was shocked by this. Following the WSPU's decision not to support Labour candidates in elections, an editorial in the ILP paper *The Labour Leader* declared, 'One would have thought that the services which the Chairman of the Party [i.e. Hardie] had rendered to women, not to speak of the Independent Labour Party as a whole ... would have met with at least some recognition'.[25] The dismal scenario of 1907 was completed by the failure, once again, of the Labour Party (extant since 1900 as a federation of labour and trade union organisations to which the ILP was affiliated) to adopt a women's suffrage resolution. The ILP, although respecting the sincerity of Hardie's views, expressed its concern at what it perceived as the tendency to subordinate all other issues to that of women's suffrage. Hardie appeared to be totally isolated and resorted to the unusual expedient of writing a 'personal statement' on 'The Labour Party and women's enfranchisement'.[26] In this he answered the charge that he placed women's suffrage before that of adult suffrage. Although supporting the latter, he none the less pointed out that:

> First there is no adult suffrage agitation and there is a 50-year-old women's enfranchisement agitation. The so-called Adult Suffrage League appears to exist for the one and only purpose of opposing the immediate enfranchisement of women ... Second, the only way whereby adult suffrage can be brought within the arena of practical politics is to agitate for the enfranchisement of women.

In the same article Hardie confronted two other contentious issues. The first was the anti-labour attitude of the women's movement, which he says is 'confined to a few women of one section of the movement' and which anyway should not lead the movement 'to desert a great principle because of the vagaries of some of its supporters'. The other issue was that of the women's suffrage bill itself which (despite the earlier surveys) was still condemned as one which would benefit propertied women only. To this his neat response was to ask why the bill was so strongly opposed by the propertied class!

Despite the wavering, the ILP conference in April 1907 re-affirmed its support for women's suffrage ('as a necessary step towards Adult Suffrage'). But the conference Chairman, Ramsay MacDonald, was highly critical of the debate on women's suffrage, particularly because (in spite of the recent rebuff of the ILP from the WSPU) it sent a message of greeting to suffragette prisoners and elected Mrs Pankhurst as an ILP delegate to the Labour Party conference. MacDonald regarded the greeting to the prisoners as 'false sentiment'. The only suffragists who are worthy of support are those who 'believe that our Labour Party is to get them the suffrage'.[27] As for the WSPU, he declared that he had never supported it 'because I believe – and do so now more than ever – that its tactics were likely to postpone women's enfranchisement'. The ILP, despite its conference decisions, was divided on its attitude to the women's suffrage campaign and this may explain why it received so little coverage for the remainder of 1907. None the less, in spite of continued misgivings about WSPU strategy after 1907 and, for some, even deeper misgivings about their campaign of violence, the ILP remained steadfast in its support for women's suffrage and condemned the harsh sentences meted out to suffragette prisoners. It had no doubts that the 1912 Franchise and Registration Bill, which proposed full manhood suffrage, was a government ploy and should be opposed. The fact that it was introduced at all was, according to the *Labour Leader*, 'testimony to the success of the women's movement, but it seeks to rob them of the fruits of their labour. There has been no agitation for Manhood Suffrage ... Men unenfranchised have been too dumb, yet their unnamed and unfelt wrongs are to be righted.'[28] This represented a remarkably advanced attitude for a party which clearly stood to gain from an extension of the male franchise. The ILP unequivocally stated that 'no measure will be acceptable which does not include both men and women'[29] and stated bluntly that any measure which failed to include women should be opposed.

The Labour Party

In 1900, the Labour Representation Committee (LRC), the embryonic Labour Party, was formed. This raised the question 'What would that Party do for women?'[30] Being a federal organisation of affiliated bodies (trade unions mainly and the ILP), its conferences were very male dominated and its leadership exclusively male. Membership was not open to individuals until 1918. The LRC had no programme of its own; a parliamentary voice was all that it offered. Its purpose, as stated at its founding conference in 1900, was simply 'to establish a distinct labour group in parliament who shall have their own whips and agree upon their own policy'. Affiliated organisations would finance their own candidates but would receive LRC backing. This approach continued after 1906, when the LRC was renamed the Labour Party. However, given that women's suffrage began to dominate the political agenda inside and outside parliament, the Labour Party was compelled to consider the issue. The by-election in the northern working-class town of Clitheroe in 1902 provided an early example of the dilemma faced by the over-cautious LRC leadership who were dragging their feet on women's suffrage. The Labour candidate in Clitheroe, David Shackleton,[31] (a weaver endorsed by his union, the Textile Factory Workers' Association) was forced, as a result of the activities of women trade unionists, to declare himself in favour of women's suffrage. The textile unions, unlike most others, had a predominantly female membership and given that unions affiliated to the LRC were required to defray a large part of the candidates' election expenses and subsequent living costs,[32] radical suffragists saw this as a very useful bargaining tool. Why, they argued, should their money, levied through their trade unions, be spent in supporting a candidate unless he supported their right to elect him. Esther Roper, secretary of the North of England Women's Suffrage Society, lost no time maximising the potential for women to use their trade unions to press home the women's suffrage message. She wrote a leaflet entitled 'The Cotton Trade Unions and the Enfranchisement of Women' in which she urged women to use their majority position in these unions in the north to make 'Women's Suffrage a Trade Union Question'.[33] Campaigning began in earnest in the cotton towns to solidify this demand by urging that the textile unions ballot their members on the issue of women's suffrage. The campaign was successful – ballots were organised and they showed clearly that women workers wanted the vote. Despite this remarkable example of the link between labour and suffrage in what could have been an organic and inclusive class approach to women's suffrage and labour representation for the mutual benefit of both, the LRC and indeed the TUC remained obdurately silent or opposed to women's suffrage. A great opportunity was thus sacrificed on the altar of male prejudice.

The Women's Movement

Alongside the growth of a mass labour movement, but separately, the movement for women's rights (including the franchise), also renewed itself. Together with the many successful campaigns on issues concerned with the right of women to receive a decent secondary and higher education and to enter (some) professions, and the right of married women to own property and to vote in municipal elections, middle-class women had, by the late nineteenth century, acquired an organised voice. The suffrage campaign was initially part of this general movement for equal rights. It had started in the late 1860s, attracting non-working-class women and had spawned many fractions and sometimes rival organisations. Whatever their differences, all the suffrage organisations up to the 1890s shared two characteristics – they were 'constitutional' and moderate in their aims and methods, and they did not extend their appeal to working-class women. Many of these organisations regrouped into the National Union of Women's Suffrage Societies (NUWSS) in 1897, a large umbrella body whose secretary was Millicent Fawcett.

All this was to change by the end of the century At a grassroots level, pioneering attempts to forge a link between suffrage and labour were being made, as we have seen, by working-class women in the textile areas of the north of England where a group of radical suffragists exercised influence in the North of England Women's Suffrage Society. Working-class women had their own organisational traditions, particularly in the textile unions in the north, and now in the Co-operative Women's Guilds and the Independent Labour Party. By the 1890s a group of women trade union activists working within the North of England Women's Suffrage Society had made considerable headway in linking the campaign for women's suffrage with grass-roots women's trade unionism. In a remarkable refutation of the class prejudices of the established suffrage societies and the gender-blind myopia of the labour movement, these 'radical suffragists' (notably Eva Gore-Booth, Sarah Reddish, Sarah Dickenson, Selina Cooper and others), consciously set about the task of forging an alliance between feminism and socialism.

They launched a suffrage petition in 1900 to be signed exclusively by women workers. This was accompanied by mass campaigning in all the factory districts.[34]

Initially, Christabel Pankhurst , despite her later repudiation of the working-class and labour movement, was active in a newly formed breakaway from the North of England Women's Suffrage Society. The new organisation, the Manchester and Salford Women's Trade Council, founded by Esther Roper, Eva Gore-Booth, Sara Dickenson and others was based on working women. Its purpose was to campaign in trade unions on women's suffrage. Although many of these women, including the Pankhursts, were ILP members, they were infuriated with the ILP's lack of commitment to women's suffrage in the early days. This, together with their frustration with the slow progress of the constitutional women's suffrage societies, led some of them to conclude that a new organisation, unaffiliated to the NUWSS, was necessary if women were to gain the vote in their lifetime. It is to this organisation that we must now turn, although it must be noted that the type of campaigning mentioned above still continued during and after the heyday of the WSPU.

2

The Women's Social and Political Union

A new suffrage organisation, the Women's Social and Political Union, was formed in 1903 at the Manchester home of the Pankhurst family. Its beginnings were fairly inauspicious, but its subsequent development attracted much attention, supporting its own later claim to be the most important of the women's suffrage societies in the twentieth century. Certainly many historians have accepted this view that the WSPU had of itself, to the extent that until recently much suffrage history has misunderstood, downplayed or even ignored the work of many of the less publicity-conscious suffrage societies. The attention given to the older and much larger National Union of Women's Suffrage Societies (NUWSS, led by Millicent Fawcett) pales into insignificance in comparison with that accorded to the WSPU, despite the fact that the former arguably played a more consistent role and that some of the suffrage societies, especially in the north west of England, which affiliated to it maintained a link with the labour movement and attracted a strong following among working-class women. Indeed, by 1912 the NUWSS itself had made an historic alliance with the Labour Party which, according to Jill Liddington 'brought about for the first time in English history the great weight of the trade union movement ... behind the demand for women's political rights'.[1]

Sylvia Pankhurst was not as involved as her mother, Emmeline or her sister, Christabel, in the work of the new organisation in its first two years. She was 21 at the time and an active member of the ILP, as were all the Pankhursts. However, despite their support for the ILP, they were aware that, at this stage anyway, it was 'no more than lukewarm on the subject of votes for women'.[2] This view was confirmed by ILP leaders like Bruce Glasier and Philip Snowden who visited the Pankhursts' home. Glasier argued that class differences were more important than those based on sex, while Snowden asserted that enfranchising women would help the conservatives. Indeed, a deeper misogynism was revealed when the family found out that the ILP branch in their area, which used the newly opened Pankhurst Hall, did not admit women members. The hall had been erected in memory of Sylvia's father, Richard, a respected socialist and suffragist who had died in 1898. Sylvia, a talented artist, had lovingly contributed to its interior decoration. According to her this local display of male chauvinism 'aroused so much indignation' that it was 'the last straw which caused Mrs Pankhurst to decide on the formation of a new organisation for women'.[3] In her autobiography, Mrs Pankhurst does not mention this issue and attributes the founding of the WSPU to the youthful impatience of Christabel, who had been much impressed by the visit of the American suffragist, Susan B. Anthony, and had opined thereafter that: 'It is unendurable to think of another generation of women wasting their lives begging for the vote. We must not lose any more time. We must act.'[4]

Christabel had concluded from her brief experience with working-class women in Manchester that it was very difficult for them 'to overcome the handicap of poverty, and the domestic cares which fettered them. Being voteless they lacked prestige.' On the other hand, 'women of a higher social rank and more education had, in a mainly working-class milieu, a sort of relative autonomy'.[5] Whilst not intended as disparaging comment at this stage, it was an early expression of what Selina Cooper (one of these 'poor working-class women' with whom Christabel briefly worked and an important labour and suffrage leader) acutely detected as 'the seeds of Christabel's impatience with the Labour Movement'.[6]

The history of the WSPU has been well documented. It was certainly a stormy one, riven with internal divisions. What concerns us here is Sylvia's view of its development. Her views are of interest not only because they provide, from a socialist perspective, an interesting contrast to accepted WSPU orthodoxy, but also because hers is an 'insider's' view and cannot be dismissed as the kind of predictable attack which might be expected from either a critical faction or a downright anti-suffrage source. Of course, as an active participant and a close relative of the two leaders, Sylvia had an uneasy time in the organisation. The struggle to reconcile her twin loyalties to socialism and to feminism proved increasingly difficult, especially when the WSPU brand of feminism showed itself to be hostile to the labour movement – a fact which not only resulted

in her expulsion from the WSPU, but also occasioned a permanent break in her relationship with her mother and elder sister.
The fact that the personal and the political coincided in a very
public manner has tended to obscure the fact that Sylvia's subsequent activities among working-class women in the East End
of London, which earned her the opprobrium of her family,
were much more consistent with the early aims of the WSPU
and not the product of a wayward younger daughter yearning
for maternal attention.[7] In fact, it was Emmeline and Christabel
who changed course, not Sylvia, although the attachment of
the two former to the labour movement, even in the early days,
was less than profound. Christabel had insisted from the outset
that the WSPU must be 'independent – non-party, non-class'.[8]

However, as the preceding chapter has shown, the WSPU did
not pioneer the link between suffrage and labour. In fact, it is
questionable as to whether, given the activities of the radical
suffragists in the north of England, there was room for another
suffrage organisation, especially one that was beginning to hold
the labour movement at arm's length. This may have been one
of the reasons for deciding to move the headquarters of the
WSPU to London in 1906. Certainly policy differences were
beginning to emerge between the radical suffragists and the
WSPU. The latter (especially Christabel) was insistent that the
campaign for the vote should override all other considerations,
whereas women like Isabella Ford, an active feminist and a
member of the National Administrative Council of the ILP, were
involved in a broad range of political issues.[9] Another and more
important reason for the move to London was the decision to
centre the campaign on Westminster and the political process
generally. This was much more in conformity with the older
pressure-group style of suffrage politics, albeit that the WSPU's
methods proved later to be very different.

Sylvia was already in London when the WSPU, and her
mother and sister, decamped to the capital. She had won a
scholarship to study at the Royal College of Art in 1904 and at
the same time 'decided to assist in starting the movement in
London'.[10] Despite her poverty, she declined payment for her
WSPU work. She cites this decision as among those which influenced her life, giving the following reason for it:

> I was not wholly in agreement with the policies and ideals of
> my sister and others who were controlling the movement,
> and whilst I did not wish to disrupt the movement by urging

other policies, I desired to preserve my independence and to remain as an unpaid worker for the cause.[11]

Naturally this observation, made so many years after, contains the wisdom of hindsight, but nevertheless it was clearly a defining moment for Sylvia and indicates that the unease she felt with the WSPU surfaced much earlier than is commonly imagined.

Women's Suffrage vs Adult Suffrage

Throughout her voluminous writings, Sylvia's unease with the WSPU centres on four key issues. The first concerns the WSPU's increasingly fraught relationship with the labour movement and with the ILP in particular, the second relates to the lack of democracy in the WSPU, and the third centres on her criticism of WSPU tactics. Underlying all of these is something even more fundamental – the nature of the suffrage demand itself. Mention has already been made of the fairly limited demands of the older suffrage societies. The WSPU was little different in policy terms, demanding the vote for women 'on the same terms as that agreed or may be accorded to men'. Suffrage on this basis would thus 'duplicate many of the anomalies and class biases of the male franchise'.[12] Given that roughly one-third of adult males remained unenfranchised after the Third Reform Act, it was not unreasonable for socialists and others to wish to remedy the obvious democratic deficit in the male suffrage entitlement. However, such a seemingly logical demand took on a controversial aspect during the period in which the campaign for women's suffrage was at its height, since it could be, and often was, counterposed to women's suffrage. Hence a covert and overt form of opposition to women's suffrage expressed itself in the demand for adult suffrage. It was used overtly by the Liberal government, especially Asquith, a leading opponent of women's suffrage, who insisted that his priority was to introduce a bill to rectify the male suffrage anomaly and that the supporters of women's suffrage would be at liberty to propose amendments to such a bill. Asquith was able to use this tactic to prevaricate, in the knowledge that the suffrage campaign was divided. Within the labour movement, whilst there was a genuine equal suffrage element truly supportive of women, there was also an anti-women's suffrage contingent which used the adult suffrage demand as a cover for their antifeminism.[13] This said, however, insufficient attention has been paid to the pro-feminist supporters of adult suffrage, who undoubtedly exercised a strong influence in sections of the labour movement and, more importantly, among working-class women. Gertrude Tuckwell, Honorary Secretary of the Women's Trade Union League, raised the issue, a year after the formation of the WSPU, in the correspondence columns of the ILP paper, *The Labour Leader.* She questioned the wisdom of the tactics of supporting a 'limited bill' because she feared that 'the admission of women to the existing male franchise would rest the franchise on so sure a basis of British Conservatism as to prevent our obtaining adult suffrage'[14] since only middle- and upper-class women would benefit.

Eva Gore-Booth, also an active trade unionist, disagreed. She thought that under a limited bill, 'many thousands of skilled women workers in the North of England ... should easily qualify themselves for the lodger franchise'.[15] On Tuckwell's party political point Gore-Booth noted that the present government 'owes its existence to staunch majorities of working men' and that anyway it was unfair to 'refuse equal rights and justice to a large section of the community simply because you are of the opinion that their votes may go to strengthen the hands of one party or another'. Ada Neild Chew, an organiser for the Women's Trade Union League in Lancashire, supported Gertrude Tuckwell's line in more forceful terms. She was indignant that Lancashire trade union women had signed petitions for a women's suffrage bill under false pretences:

> not one in a hundred knows that the Bill would not give them a vote if passed. This has been kept from them. The Bill is a class and property Bill, and we have enough property franchises already. A vote for women by all means, but when we get it let us see that the *working women* – the women who earn their daily bread by their daily toil, and the mothers who *are* rearing our future citizens – shall be considered *first*, and not last.'[16]

A public debate in 1907 on the rival strategies of adult versus women's suffrage between two genuine supporters of sex equality survives as a record of the difficult tactical choices faced by feminists on this important issue.[17] The debate was between Teresa Billington Greig (ex WSPU, now of the Women's Freedom League) and Margaret Bondfield (Assistant

Secretary of the Shop Assistants' Union and President of the Adult Suffrage Society). It was chaired by Isabella Ford (ILP) who, in introducing the debate, declared that its purpose was to decide 'whether it would be better to alter the existing basis of the franchise and bring in Adult suffrage, or whether the quickest way to obtain Adult suffrage ... is to destroy sex disability first'.[18] Billington Greig argued that sex disability was the most fundamental question of all and that removing it over-rode all other considerations – obtaining it would be just 'even if only half a dozen women were enfranchised'.[19] She estimated that two million women would be enfranchised (compared with 7.5 million men) if the vote was accorded to them on the basis of the existing male suffrage law. This, she argued, would benefit more women than was commonly supposed and would enfranchise some working-class women. However, whilst acknowledging that many working-class women would still be excluded, she justified this on the basis of the principle of equality; 'I want an equal recognition even if it is limited, or if it is not quite so fair as it might be, because of the wrong conditions which men have made.' It was wrong to ask women to wait until men had 'mended their own bad franchise conditions',[20] conditions which she later condemned as stupid, illog ical and undemocratic. But, she asked, if men use this flawed franchise, why can't women? Furthermore, she questioned the motives of the proponents of adult suffrage since she suspected that they were using this demand as a cover for manhood suffrage and that once they had obtained this they would 'ditch' the women. In her reply, Margaret Bondfield disputed much of the detail of Billington Greig's assessment of the effect of the extension of the existing franchise on working-class women. Her view was that far fewer women workers would benefit and she was particularly concerned at the impact of the exclusion of married women. She argued that women who wanted the franchise on the same terms as men had the perfect right to campaign for it 'but don't let them come and tell me that they are working for my class'.[21] In fact, she suspected the motives of the middle class supporters of a 'limited bill'. They were using the demand as 'an effective barrier' to what anti-socialists regarded as 'the dangerous demand for adult suffrage'. Later in the debate Bondfield was critical of the stance of the labour movement on the suffrage question and agreed that they 'have not been so active as they might be'. However, those in the labour movement were now 'beginning to understand that they cannot progress with their ideals until they have the women marching side by side with them'.[22]

It is difficult to know precisely the point at which Sylvia became critical of the long-accepted women's suffrage demand drafted by her father in the late 1860s. There is no record of her opposition to it prior to 1914, but her later writings suggest that she regarded it as profound tactical error from as early as 1906 for two reasons. First, because the women's movement's rejection of adult suffrage fuelled the rift between it and the labour movement. As she states in *The Suffragette Movement*:

> In the light of later events, it is now obvious that a grave mistake was made in leaving the field of adult suffrage – the true field of the Labour Movement – to those who were either hostile or indifferent to the inclusion of women ... Had other councils prevailed then, the Labour Party might have given a great lead for a Manhood and Womanhood Suffrage Reform Bill.[23]

Second, she regarded the precise nature of the women's suffrage 'magic incantation' as 'no longer appropriate after 1906'[24] since it was undemocratic and exclusive. A bill based on traditional demand would give votes only to 'propertied spinsters and widows' and hence (with some justice), Asquith and Lloyd George smeared it as a 'ladies' bill'. In addition she noted with some sympathy that 'the Labour Party did not like a bill which would leave out manual workers'.[25] Much later, reminiscing on how the vote was won, she expressed an even more forthright criticism of the suffrage demand. She wrote:

> In those days no-one dared to ask for the vote for every woman. Right up to the end the suffrage societies, with the sole exception of my own East London Federation ... worked for little bills to enfranchise less than 10% of us, and at many stages they actually proposed to exclude married women altogether.[26]

Such misgivings over so fundamental an issue, even though they may have been stifled in the cause of women's unity, are indicative of something much more than a personal dilemma. They capture the complexities of the competing loyalties of socialism and feminism in the context of the imperfections of both movements. Sylvia was not alone in attempting to reconcile these twin loyalties, but she was unique within the WSPU. It meant that she was constantly swimming against the tide of the organisation to which she owed deep personal and family loyalty. It is hardly surprising, then, that she was highly critical of developments within the WSPU which distanced it from the labour movement.

The WSPU and the Labour Movement

Sylvia was acutely aware of the anti-feminist imperfections of the labour movement and was unafraid to fight against them, but her standpoint was always one of a critical insider. She recognised that the women's movement had staunch and principled supporters in the ILP, none more so than her great friend, Keir Hardie. Unlike her mother and sister, she also recognised that the battle to win hearts and minds within a male-dominated movement was inevitably uphill, but vital none the less because votes for women was not an end in itself, but a means of achieving social justice for all. She was deeply concerned throughout her life with the plight of super-exploited working-class women. She was aware that lives of working men were hard, 'but the condition of women is indeed terrible. Who can fail to connect this with their unenfranchised state?'[27] For her, therefore, the issue of the women's franchise was a class question and meant that it had perforce to be an issue for the labour movement and vice versa. She viewed with alarm the growing coolness shown to the Labour Party and the ILP by the WSPU, all the more shocking to Sylvia in view of her family's long-standing connections with the socialist movement. Her mother had been instrumental in getting the ILP to adopt women's suffrage as a policy and had encouraged Selina Cooper to second a similar motion proposed by the Amalgamated Society of Engineers at the 1905 Labour Party conference.[28] The motion was wrecked by a hostile adult suffrage amendment proposed by Harry Quelch of the SDF. This was a setback, but did not warrant the refusal of the WSPU to support the Labour candidate (who was a strong supporter of women's suffrage) in the Huddersfield by-election of 1906. Worse was to come. In 1907 Christabel issued a press statement formalising the WSPU position, which asserted that her organisation made no distinction between the Conservative, Liberal and Labour Parties. Whilst it is true that the 1907 Labour Party conference once again adopted an adultist resolution, this can hardly be seen as a justification for the decision of Christabel and Emmeline Pankhurst to leave the ILP in that year. After all, the ILP had been committed to women's suffrage since 1905, even if the Labour Party was not. Sylvia's view was somewhat ambivalent. On one hand she argued that patient work needed to be done in order to get the Labour Party to change its position. The main obstacle to this was both the hostile attitude of the WSPU and the fact that the nature of their limited suffrage demand, which would have enfranchised only one woman in thirteen, gave succour to the adultist position. On the other hand she was, at the same time, dismayed to the point of permanent pessimism by the 1907 Labour Party conference decision, which she felt 'precluded the Party from doing anything to advance either women's suffrage on the present terms, or adult manhood and womanhood suffrage'.[29] In the same passage she quotes Frederick Pethick-Lawrence's view as expressed in *The Labour Record* that the Labour Party decision meant 'the final severance of the woman's movement from the Labour Movement'. As she struggled to reconcile, as a socialist, her understanding of the vicissitudes in the development of fledgling labour politics with an understandable impatience with the Party's attitude to women, the leadership of the WSPU brought the issue to a head. The rift between the WSPU and the labour movement was complete and final in 1907. Sylvia suggests that the break was unconnected with the fateful 1907 conference decision. Time and again she alludes to the fact that Christabel had never been truly committed to labour movement politics and that, in fact (according to Sylvia), she viewed the alliance with labour as a nuisance. She (i.e. Christabel) 'would not brook a divided allegiance: she wanted to build a body of women caring for no other public question save the vote'[30] and to achieve this it was necessary 'to stimulate the growth of a large non-party body, and to attract especially the support of wealthy Conservatives opposed to Labour views'.[31] To press the point home, members of the WSPU were called on to sign a pledge undertaking 'not to support the candidates of any political party at Parliamentary elections until women have the vote'.[32] This must have posed a huge dilemma for Sylvia, who solved it by refusing to sign the pledge, but at the same time did not contravene it. Her loyalty was tested to its limits when she was called upon to implement Christabel's policy at a by-election at Bury St Edmunds. She describes her embarrassment at having to toe the WSPU line in opposing the Liberal candidate and being thus presumed to support the Tory (a member of the Guinness family). She was upbraided by Christabel when it was reported that she had informed a public meeting that she was a socialist and that she did not welcome a Tory victory. In the light of the these difficulties it is hardly surprising that she withdrew temporarily from WSPU activity. She went to Cradley Heath in 1907 and was only prevailed upon to return to London when summoned by Christabel, who wanted her to attend a members' meeting called to deal with an oppositional minority within the WSPU.

The Democratic Deficit in the WSPU

Differences within the WSPU led, in 1907, to the formation of a breakaway organisation, the Women's Freedom League (WFL). The opponents of the Pankhurst leadership, Edith How Martyn, Teresa Billington Greig and the veteran suffrage activist, Charlotte Despard, were regarded by Sylvia as having few, if any, policy differences with the WSPU. The issue rather centred on the lack of democracy within the WSPU. Sylvia had already noted the autocratic style of the Pankhurst leadership, which, after the split with Labour, regarded the WSPU as an army in battle over which they had supreme control. Any questioning of the command of the generals was tantamount to mutiny. As Christabel later wrote: 'It was as though in the midst of a battle, the Army had begun to vote on who should command it and what the strategy should be.'[33] This is a reference to the High Command's decision to abolish the democratic constitution of the WSPU, which in turn meant abandoning the annual delegate conference. It was to this that the 'mutineers' of the as yet unformed WFL objected and as a consequence held their own conference on the date previously scheduled for that of the WSPU. Discipline became even tighter after this incident, as did the sectarianism of the WSPU. This is revealed in the decision to start a new WSPU paper *Votes For Women. Women's Franchise*, the main women's suffrage paper, published independently by J. E. Francis, had offered space to all the suffrage groups. After 1907, space was also offered to the new WFL. This was entirely unacceptable to the WSPU leadership, who by now regarded their organisation as the only worthy one. Certainly by 1908 relationships with the NUWSS were at rock bottom, for reasons to be dealt with later.

It becomes increasingly difficult to understand, given her own criticisms of the WSPU and her socialist politics, why Sylvia remained in the organisation for as long as she did. Certainly the situation did not get any easier for her. On the contrary, the autocracy was so stifling that it was capable of turning upon and purging even the closest personal friends, as the Pethick-Lawrences' case showed. Frederick and Emmeline Pethick-Lawrence had been closely associated with the suffrage question for as long as Mrs Pankhurst. They were her contemporaries and had been particularly generous to Christabel in providing her with a comfortable home in London in the early years of the WSPU. As a wealthy couple, they had contributed large sums of money to the organisation and both of them had been tried together with Mrs Pankhurst for conspiracy and sentenced to nine months' imprisonment. They were part of the top leadership of the WSPU until 1912, when they were summarily expelled because they had raised doubts about the new campaign of arson which had been launched while the couple were in Canada. This was a cruel blow. Frederick Pethick-Lawrence, in a letter to George Lansbury, expressed their feelings thus: 'the situation has nearly stunned us. To be asked to leave the WSPU to which we have contributed our life blood, was like a mother being asked to part from her little child.'[34]

Emmeline Pethick-Lawrence says in her autobiography that after the expulsion she never saw or heard from Mrs Pankhurst or Christabel again, although she (and her husband) maintained friendly contact with Sylvia. In a letter from Mrs Pethick-Lawrence to Sylvia written many years later, the former provides an interesting assessment of Mrs Pankhurst's character. She regards her former friend 'dispassionately... as an interesting human problem'.[35] She views her as a Napoleon-like character with a historical mission which in the end 'obsessed her like a passion'. In order to obtain her goal 'she threw scruple, affection, honour, loyalty and her own principles to the winds'. She goes on:

> The movement developed her powers – all her powers for good and evil. Cruelty and ruthlessness ... [next few words are illegible] ... I should add betrayal ... She was capable of beautiful tenderness and magnificent sense of justice and self-sacrifice. These things in the course of the struggle become changed. We all sacrifice many things – she sacrificed her very soul.

The letter was written after Mrs Pankhurst's death and shortly before the unveiling of her statue outside the House of Commons. It represents an attempt to understand and lay to rest the pain (shared by both correspondents) of the past in which the personal and the political had collided with such wounding repercussions.

The Pethick-Lawrences, together with some other disaffected former WSPU stalwarts (like Evelyn Sharp), formed their own organisation in 1914, the United Suffragists. They took over the former WSPU paper, *Votes for Women*.[36]

WSPU 'Terrorism'

Sylvia's writings (although not her actions), show that she was strongly opposed to the change in the tactics of the WSPU. Impatience with the lack of progress of the suffrage demand and demoralised by the known anti-suffrage line of Asquith, who had become the Liberal Prime Minister in 1908, induced Christabel into launching, in 1909, a campaign of direct action which involved window-breaking and, later, more serious acts of criminal damage to public and private property, courting the arrest and imprisonment of the perpetrators. This phase of the WSPU campaign attracted widespread publicity, not least because it led to the martyrdom of individuals who underwent the privations of prison and hunger strike in the service of the cause. Hunger strikers were forcibly fed. Though reviled in their day, these women, the suffragette 'militants', have been more honoured by posterity than the less publicity-conscious foot soldiers. The uneasy tension between admiration for individual bravery and unease at an individualistic strategy, which at its height bordered on mindless violence, is found in Sylvia's writings. She profoundly disagreed with the movement's new direction because she 'did not think the old methods had been exploited to their full capacity' and that 'the movement required not more serious militancy by the few, but a stronger appeal to the masses to join the struggle'.[37] However, she goes on to say that she would 'rather have died at the stake than criticize the actions of the militants'. We must assume from this that she probably did not voice her criticisms at the time. She was sufficiently alienated from the leadership for her views to have made little difference and was in America on a speaking tour from December 1911 to March 1912. None the less, her own frequent spells of imprisonment and hunger striking from 1912 onwards indicate that her critical attitude was not born of personal cowardice. In fact, she went on hunger (and on two occasions thirst and sleep) strikes and endured forcible feeding more times than almost anyone.[38] Much later, in an unpublished reflection of the women's movement, she is even more critical of 'secret militancy', even referring to it as terrorism:

> Secretly planned militancy was a method of desperation adopted in the hope of shortening the longer struggle ... I must confess that these particular tactics never appealed to me. I took no part in them. I thoroughly disliked the destruction of works of art. I did not then and I do not now express one word of censure upon the brave women who were secret militants. They acted ... largely at the instigation of my sister Christabel and my mother ... my sister ... declared that, without an element of real terrorism, the Government would never grant women the franchise.[39]

She goes on to say that such tactics were not only incorrect and ineffective but that they 'retarded a wonderful movement which ... was rising towards a great climax when secret militancy was introduced'. This tactic, in Sylvia's opinion, 'tended to dilute enthusiasm by introducing new elements of doubt' about suffrage methods.

Given all these fundamental disagreements with WSPU tactics and strategy, Sylvia's decision in 1912 to establish the East London Federation of Suffragettes (ELFS) was hardly surprising. It represented a practical attempt to pursue the kind of women's suffrage campaign which the parent organisation had, by this time, clearly rejected. However, it was not the only course open to her. The East London Federation (as it was then called) was, until 1914, part of the WSPU and might well have remained so had it and Sylvia not been expelled. Given her commitment to socialist principles, to links with the labour movement and to democratic mass campaigning, it is surprising that she at best bypassed and at worse ignored the important developments (discussed below) that had taken place within the other mass suffrage organisation, the NUWSS, which by 1912 had resulted in the unique labour suffrage alliance. She notes that in 1907 the NUWSS was 'waking from a long inertia'[40] a somewhat unfair comment given the activities of its working-class women members in the north of England.

The NUWSS and the Labour-Suffrage Alliance

The NUWSS seems to have hit a sectarian blind-spot in Sylvia's thinking. Mention has already been made of the activities of the radical suffragists in the north of England and the mass involvement of working-class women in the campaign for the vote. There is little in Sylvia's writings about this, nor about the alliance between the NUWSS and the Labour Party which existed in a practical form between 1912 and 1914. Until 1908, relations between the WSPU and the NUWSS had been cordial. After that year, however, the violent tactics of the WSPU induced a complete break between the two organisations. The NUWSS was openly critical of the new departure and viewed WSPU militants as criminals rather than as martyrs. Millicent Fawcett's reason for condemning the WSPU would not have commended itself to Sylvia, despite the latter's own reservations about the campaign of violence. Fawcett wrote:

> The House of Commons with all its faults, stands for order against anarchy, for justice against brutality, and to overcome it by brute force of the lowest ruffians in London was in my opinion the act of a mad women or a dastard. It became evident to me that our organisation must separate itself entirely from all co-operation with people who would resort to such weapons ... The crimes committed in Ireland by the Home Rulers stopped Home Rule and if women suffragists embark on crime as propaganda, they will stop women's suffrage.[41]

Whatever her own misgivings about WSPU tactics, Sylvia was unlikely to ally herself with this kind of moderate constitutionalist position. None the less, such statements belied the fact that the NUWSS was changing rapidly. It had undergone a spectacular growth after 1911, when it had 30,000 members. This figure rose to 42,000 a year later (by which time it employed 61 paid organisers) and had reached 53,000 by 1914.[42] The defeat of the Conciliation Bill in 1912 led to a momentous change. It induced the NUWSS to abandon all hope in the Liberal Party and turn instead to the Labour Party. An Election Fighting Fund was established with the express aim of supporting Labour candidates who were standing against Liberal anti-suffragists. This was a bold departure for an organisation which had, until now, been steadfastly non-political. In fact, as Leslie Parker Hume[43] points out, it alienated many of the NUWSS's respectable middle-class, Liberal Party-inclined members. This was more than compensated for by a successful drive to court working-class women. This entailed propaganda work in trade unions in order to ensure that, as paymasters of the Labour Party, their influence would not be used to weaken the Party's more robust stance on women's suffrage. When, in 1913, the Speaker of the House of Commons announced that, contrary to previous assurances, a women's suffrage amendment would *not* be taken to the current Reform Bill, the Labour Party conference of that year declared that it would oppose any franchise bill which failed to include women. This was an enormous step forward and was backed by a resolution of the 1913 TUC, which called 'upon the Parliamentary Committee to press for the immediate enfranchisement of women'.[44] Hence, as Liddington argues, the result of the Labour-suffrage alliance was to bring about 'for the first time in English history the great weight of the trade union movement ... behind the demand for women's political rights'.[45] It was as though the fight by women textile workers, launched in 1902 during the Clitheroe by-election, to force the labour movement to fight for its women members had finally been won. Whilst the WSPU was engaged in bombing Lloyd George's house and similar stunts, no one in that organisation, not even Sylvia, appeared to notice that the original intention of the WSPU's founders – that of a Labour-suffrage alliance – was now a practical reality.

Of course, the fact that the WSPU leadership had explicitly departed from its founding strategy many years earlier explains the deafening silence on the part of the organisation. It is, however, not so easy to explain Sylvia's position. It may be that, although critical of the WSPU, she was still a member of it and felt that she owed it some loyalty, publicly at least. In one of her few utterances on the Labour-suffrage alliance she seemed distinctly lukewarm and characterised it as 'putting the cart before the horse'.[46] In addition, she shared the historic intolerance of the constitutional suffrage society and of Mrs Fawcett in particular. After all, impatience with its long-standing moderate position had been the chief reason for the formation of the WSPU in the first place. Based in London, it may have been difficult for her to appreciate the slow but steady changes that working-class women in the north had wrought within the NUWSS. By 1912, when the alliance with Labour came into force, the development of a mass labour movement had spawned a new brand of syndicalist militancy and Sylvia was caught up with the radical rank-and-file challenge to what was perceived as a reformist incorporated Labour Party. In common with others on the left, her impatience with the official movement may perhaps be offered as an additional explanation for her disregard of the Labour-suffrage alliance. However, much later, in 1921, she invoked the spirit of Keir Hardie to legitimise her anti-NUWSS position. She claimed that:

> he advised the National Union of Women's Suffrage Societies against supporting Labour Party candidates financially, and otherwise telling them that their wisest course was to run their own independent campaign ... he was not unmindful of the anti-socialist tendencies that might come into the Party through the influence of a party of women who were merely suffragists and almost entirely animated by bourgeois ideology.[47]

Whatever the reason for her disinterest in the Labour-suffrage alliance, the fact was that Sylvia was deeply involved in her own world of suffrage/socialist politics to which, in 1912, she was about to give practical expression in the East End of London.

3

The East End, the First World War and the Revolutionary Tide

Sylvia's decision to form a suffrage organisation in the East End of London was not motivated solely by her frustration with the WSPU, but more positively by her desire to create a mass women's movement. Only in such a movement 'could the gage be taken ... which history itself had flung to us' and this would be accomplished 'not by the secret militancy of a few enthusiasts, but by the rising of the masses'.[1] She chose the East End because

> it was the greatest homogenous working class area accessible to the House of Commons by popular demonstrations. The creation of a woman's [sic] movement in that great abyss of poverty would be a call and a rallying cry to the rise of similar movements in all parts of the country.[2]

She was aware that the WSPU had become a predominantly middle-class organisation and that its hostility to the Labour Party was deeply resented in working-class areas. Hence her objective was 'the building up of a movement independent in method and ideals from that in which my mother and my sister were engaged'.[3] Moreover, she felt that the traditional women's suffrage demand was perceived by women workers as a 'vote for ladies'. She wanted working-class women to be fighters on their own account, free from the patronising attitudes of middle-class women which however well intentioned, served to place women workers in the role of victims, thereby undermining their potential to liberate themselves. But how could Sylvia, as a middle-class woman herself, avoid the same charge? After all, she was an alien incomer to the East End and as such had a mode of speech and manner that differed markedly from the resident population. Anyone who knows the East End will be aware that, as in most close working-class communities (much closer then than now), there was a deep mistrust of 'toffs'. Whilst successive waves of immigrants (the latest being Jews

36

fleeing from persecution in Eastern Europe) lent the area a cos-
mopolitan atmosphere, its class character remained unchanged,
as did the poverty and social deprivation of its inhabitants. It is
remarkable that Sylvia was accepted so quickly within the area
and that she succeeded in attracting a group of local women
into her organisation which, although initially small, eventually resulted, by 1917, in the formation of 30 branches
nationwide (the majority in the East End[4]), capable of mobilising thousands of women. Thus in a short period Sylvia had
established a firm base in the East End which enabled the
under-rated intelligence and organisational skills of working-
class women to be fully utilised on their own account. Such
women, like Mrs Parsons, Charlotte Drake, Melvina Walker,
Julia Scurr, Annie Barnes, Nellie Cressall and others,were all
from poor East-End families and yet found the time to involve
themselves in suffrage and anti-war work. They formed a solid
base around which the movement was built in East London.
Unfortunately, as is so often the case with working-class women
'hidden from history', very little is known about their lives and
they themselves were far too busy and self-effacing to leave
much in the way of written records. Nellie Cressall, however,
left some papers which remain in the safe keeping of her family.
She was, later, a councillor in Poplar and was imprisoned in
1921 when the majority of Poplar councillors, in protest against
an unequal rating system led by George Lansbury, refused to
levy the Poplar rate.[5] Nellie Cressall described her reasons for
joining the suffrage campaign and the influence on her of Sylvia:

> In 1912 I met Sylvia and others. I had been thinking for some
> time of the unequal rights of men and women. I could not
> agree that men should be the sole parent, that a mother
> could not even say whether her child should be vaccinated or
> not – or that women should receive half pay and many other
> things as well ... after talking to Sylvia and other speakers I
> thought that here is something I can dedicate myself to help
> in some way to put things right.[6]

Hence the motivation of Nellie Cressall, and many of her group,
was not the vote alone. They had a wider vision of women's
emancipation based on their daily experiences of economic and
social inequality.

   In addition to an existing working-class feminist consciousness in the East End, Sylvia was also able to build on an already

existing suffrage work. In 1906, a branch of the WSPU had been formed in the East End's Canning Town, largely on the initiative of the socialist Dora Montefiore.[7] In fact, there had been consistent suffrage work in the East End from 1906–12, with other branches having been formed in Bow and Poplar. These branches were unpopular with the WSPU leadership, especially after 1907 when Mrs Pankhurst and Christabel had broken with the Labour Party. The East-End women remained strongly pro-labour, involved themselves in the labour movement and demanded votes for all women without property qualification. It is hardly surprising that the WSPU leadership virtually ignored these East-End branches. Sylvia herself paid scant attention to this development, dating 1912 as the beginning of suffrage work in the area.[8]

The existence of WSPU branches before 1912 does not detract from Sylvia's subsequent achievement in the East End. It was, and always had been, clear to her that the East End was fertile territory for the development of a working women's movement with a socialist perspective which would be allied to the labour movement. This outlook, together with the democratic involvement of its members, helps to explain the success of the new organisation. The East London Federation of the WSPU (ELF) was from its inception led and run by East End women. Sylvia played a leading role together with two other 'outsiders', Nora Smyth and an American, Zelie Emerson, but none of them dominated. At the same time, Sylvia did not patronise either. She did not descend as a missionary 'do-gooder' – she fought for her line politically through a democratic structure. Founded as it was during the height of the 'great unrest' it aligned itself from the outset with the issues and campaigns of the left wing of the labour movement. It saw the vote as an instrument of social change and not an end in itself. As Sylvia put it, the East End movement was 'not merely for votes but towards an egalitarian society – an effort to awaken the women submerged in poverty to struggle for better social conditions and bring them into line with the most advanced sections of the movement of the awakened proletariat'.[9]

Expulsion

Needless to say, the WSPU leadership was hostile to these developments; the only surprise, given the autocratic and increasingly right-wing nature of the parent body, was that the expulsion of the East London Federation did not take place until 1914. Sylvia saw the 'breach widening: my relatives were moving to the right and our Federation to the left'.[10] The ELF maintained a strong agitation for the vote, although its tactics differed from the WSPU, preferring as it did the use of mass mobilisation rather than individual acts of violence. There was, none the less, a strong hint of WSPU tactics in Sylvia's and Zelie Emerson's stone-throwing activities (twice in February 1913) which resulted in their arrest and, on the second occasion, imprisonment.[11] The influence of WSPU militarism can be seen in the formation of the People's Army in 1913 – 'an organisation men and women may join in order to fight for freedom ... in order that they may fit themselves to cope with the brutality of government servants'.[12] Sylvia acknowledged that the term 'army' was ' rhetorical rather than militaristic',[13] despite the fact that Sir Francis Vane had offered to provide army officers to drill the volunteers. However, neither of these two tactical hangovers detracted from the genuinely democratic nature of the ELF and the mass support it generated. Given the militant climate of the times generally, such tactics did not seem as adventurist as they might be judged in altered circumstances.

Two major clashes between the WSPU and the ELF took place before the final rift. The first was in November 1912 when, at the height of the suffrage agitation, George Lansbury, the MP for Bow and Bromley, resigned his seat in order to fight a by-election on the issue of women's suffrage. Lansbury briefly became the hero of the women's suffrage movement and his decision to fight an election on this single issue alone commended him to the WSPU, who fully supported his campaign, (as did the NUWSS) and sent in helpers to canvass the constituency. At last, it would appear that a WSPU-labour alliance had been born and that Sylvia's organisation was about to find favour with the parent body (in both senses of the word!). This was not the case. Sylvia regarded Lansbury's decision as 'rash and premature',[14] first because she felt that the East End lagged behind the industrial north in its support for women's suffrage, and second because he had not consulted the local constituency party which felt that it had been 'bounced' into an unwelcome election.[15] Lansbury had paid more heed to WSPU counsels (especially that of Christabel) than to that of the labour movement. Thus, when an army of middle-class suffragettes descended on the constituency they were met with a wall of hostility from local activists, most of whom disapproved of

WSPU politics anyway. Hence, despite some well-attended public meetings, canvassing was poorly organised. Sylvia's more fundamental criticism of Lansbury concerned her opposition to his tactics within the parliamentary Labour Party. He had taken the line advocated by the WSPU that Labour should oppose all government measures unless and until Asquith's cabinet introduced and supported a women's franchise bill. Lansbury presumably thought that this 'principled' position would be a vote winner, since he made much of it in his election address in which he criticised his own party's position on women's suffrage:

> The only effective method by which we can prevent the women of this country being left out of the next Franchise Bill, is for a sufficient number of men in the House of Commons ... to inform the Government that they will not continue their support for other measures unless this reform is absolutely secured and passed into law as a Government measure.[16]

Hardie, who was equally committed to the cause of women's suffrage, took a different position. He urged opposition to the current Reform Bill at all its parliamentary stages, but realised that blanket opposition to the government would put the Labour Party in the invidious position of opposing measures with which it agreed, prime amongst which was Home Rule for Ireland.[17] This, for Sylvia, was a more principled position, although it incurred the wrath of the WSPU who lampooned Hardie in *The Suffragette* as being a poodle of Asquith. For the WSPU the only issue was the vote and, as Christabel pronounced in *The Suffragette*, this was far more important than the Irish question.[18] Thus, far from cementing the Labour-suffrage alliance, Lansbury's campaign, which ended in failure, damaged it still further without bringing tangible results to the women's cause other than short-lived publicity. Presumably this explains why the result did not matter to Christabel. Writing from her safe refuge in Paris, she expressed the view that 'whatever the result the fight has been gloriously worthwhile and has done untold good'.[19] Once the election was over the WSPU decamped from the East End, adding further fuel to the prevalent opinion that they had used the local community as an election stunt and were not in the least interested in the plight of working-class women.

The WSPU's brief flirtation with Lansbury ended after the election campaign. So long as he was prepared to repudiate every other issue save the vote he was an ally. But Lansbury was a socialist and the editor of the *Daily Herald*. In the turbulent years prior to the First World War he was bound to be involved in other causes. In 1913, under the auspices of the Herald League, a mass rally was organised in the Albert Hall in support of the workers involved in the famous Dublin lockout and to demand the release from prison of James Larkin of the Irish Transport and General Workers' Union, one of the most prominent trade union leaders in Ireland. James Connolly was a speaker at the rally, as was Sylvia. Attended by over 10,000 people, the rally was significant, according to Dangerfield, because it was 'the first and last time Irish Nationalism, Militant Suffrage, and the Labour Unrest were met together'.[20] Sylvia's appearance on the platform led to a huge row with the WSPU leadership (described by Sylvia as 'a storm in a tea cup'[21]) in which she was accused of entering into an alliance with the Herald League. Christabel, from her exile in Paris, wrote two furious letters to Sylvia. In the first she revealed that she had refused Lansbury's personal request for a WSPU speaker for the rally[22] and in the second she condemned Sylvia's decision to speak in the name of the WSPU in tones which clearly presaged the forthcoming expulsion. She wrote: 'it is essential for the public to understand that you are working independently of us ... As you have complete confidence in your own policy and way of doing things, this should suit you perfectly.'[23] Sylvia issued a circular expressly repudiating the charge that she had made an alliance with the Herald League, although she wrote to Lansbury apologising for any impression that this might create that the ELF be regarded as 'ungracious towards our good men friends down here'.[24] None the less, she was unapologetic about her decision to speak, since she was convinced that she was right 'to keep our working women's movement in touch with the main body of the working-class movement'.[25] Clearly the WSPU intended to make this into a big issue. Indeed, Sylvia alleges that Christabel later gave the Albert Hall meeting as the reason for the expulsion of the ELF.[26] Christabel's letters were followed by a sharp rebuke from Annie Kenney, who justified the non-participation of the WSPU leadership in the rally on the grounds that 'there are more important activities for them than platform work' and that anyway such decisions are made by Mrs Pankhurst and Christabel to whom the rest of the WSPU looked 'for guidance in the constructive and political work of the WSPU.

We know from what source all the political wisdom and marvellous insight which inspires our union, comes.'[27] It was hardly possible to have a rational discussion faced with such slavish loyalty. Within two months of this 'storm in a tea cup', the ELF, together with its founder, had been expelled from the WSPU.

The report of the expulsion in the ELF minute books provides a surprisingly dispassionate and, as far as we know, accurate contemporary account. A much fuller version of the story is contained in *The Suffragette Movement* which, whilst it does not differ substantially from the contemporary record, contains much in the way of reported speech, the accuracy of which cannot be fully verified given that it was written almost 20 years later. In January 1914 Sylvia was summoned to see Christabel in Paris. She had just been released from Holloway Prison and was, as she put it, 'miserably ill in body, and distressed by the reason of my journey'.[28] She was faced by her obdurate sister and mother, who demanded that the ELF should become a separate organisation. The meeting was clearly a painful one since it finalised not only a breach between the two organisations, but brought about a permanent fissure within the Pankhurst family. Sylvia had almost no contact with her mother and sister after this. Sylvia's companion on the Paris trip, Nora Smyth, now the financial secretary of the ELF, had once served as Mrs Pankhurst's unpaid chauffeur and was distantly related to Dr Ethel Smyth,[29] a loyal supporter of the WSPU leaders. Christabel, nursing a small Pomeranian dog, told her sister that the issue was quite simple. There could only be one locus of power in the suffragette movement and that it could brook no independent unsanctioned activity, especially from a group based on working-class women. Such women were the weakest and thus of no value to a movement which had, perforce, to be based on the strongest and most intelligent who would 'take their instructions and walk in step like an army'.[30] According to Sylvia's account, Mrs Pankhurst was distressed by the discussion and was about to offer a financial settlement to the ELF, which had raised a considerable amount of money for the parent body. However, she was over-ruled by Christabel, who insisted on a 'clean cut' and no compensation.

The Paris meeting was, of course, reported to the ELF committee. The committee was informed of the WSPU leadership's view of the main differences between the two organisations in the following terms:

We had more faith in what could be done by stirring up working women ... where they had most faith in what could be done for the vote by people of means and influence. In other words they said that they were working from the top down and we from the bottom up.[31]

In March 1914 the first issue of the *Woman's Dreadnought*, the weekly paper owned and edited by Sylvia, referred to the expulsion in somewhat more personal terms:

Some people say that the lives of working women are too hard and their education too small for them to become a powerful voice in winning the vote. Such people have forgotten their history.[32]

The British press, in an effort to capitalise on the split, concluded erroneously that it had occurred because Sylvia would not accept the WSPU's decision to order a temporary truce from militancy. Christabel issued a statement correcting this in which she baldly stated that WSPU's 'word of command is given by Mrs. Pankhurst and myself ... Consequently those who wish to give an independent lead ... must necessarily have an independent organisation of their own.'[33]

There is one discrepancy between Sylvia's later account and the contemporary record. In the former Sylvia suggests that when ELF members were informed of the WSPU leadership's decision they refused to accept it and would not change the name of their organisation. The minutes, however, record that a local woman, Mrs Parsons, proposed that a separate organisation was entirely appropriate on the grounds that 'they [i.e. the WSPU] are the West End: we are the East End' and that Sylvia 'would be leader down here'.[34] And thus it was: the East London Federation of the WSPU was now renamed the East London Federation of the Suffragettes (ELFS), much to the annoyance of Mrs Pankhurst, and adopted the WSPU colours of purple, green and white, with the addition of red. Within a couple of months it had established its own paper, the *Woman's Dreadnought*.[35] The cut was to be 'cleaner' than Christabel, or anyone else for that matter, could possibly have anticipated.

The demand for votes for women had acquired widespread support prior to the outbreak of the First World War. The labour movement had been won over. Within the Liberal Party the supporters of women's franchise were more vocal, and this undoubtedly had an impact on Asquith who, in June 1914, had agreed to meet an ELFS suffrage deputation. Sylvia had forced his hand by declaring, at the end of May, that she would embark on an indefinite hunger, thirst and sleep strike inside and outside prison unless he agreed to meet this deputation. The deputation was a remarkable one not only because it was one of the very few that Asquith agreed to meet, but also because it consisted of six working-class women from the East End who not only put the case for the vote, but described the misery of poverty and the hardship of their working lives.[36] The *Manchester Guardian* was impressed by the unique nature of this deputation which brought out the sharp contrast between 'the average poor woman's argument for enfranchisement and the average rich man's argument against it'.[37] Asquith told the deputation that he thought women's suffrage could not be delayed much longer, a sentiment supported by the Liberal press the following day. Dangerfield goes so far as to argue that this deputation more than anything else was responsible for inducing Asquith and his cabinet to give up the battle against women's suffrage.[38] In addition, it was also clear that the ELFS was also supported by male workers in the East End. A contemporary account of the huge suffrage rally (preceded by a march starting at the ELFS office in Old Ford Road) in Canning Town Hall in July 1914 is contained in the *Christian Commonwealth*, an unusual source for reports on suffrage activity, but clearly the event impressed it enough to report that:

> Quite half the audience were men, vocal and emphatic in their approval of the aims of the meeting – all types of men, but chiefly workers, many of them Socialist and trade unionists, and the majority of them rather rebellious about orthodox politics.[39]

The First World War

The outbreak of the First World War in 1914 propelled the WSPU away from feminism in favour of patriotism. It suspended its activities on the suffrage in order to focus attention on the war effort, leaving the ELFS as the most notable group in the suffrage campaign. However the ELFS was not the only suffrage organisation after 1914. Sandra Holton[40] notes that by 1914 militant suffrage forces were in the process of reforming and that 'Sylvia Pankhurst's East London Federation was not the isolated breakaway from the WSPU it might appear'.[41]

Christabel returned from her self-imposed exile in Paris to campaign against the 'German Peril'. She, her mother and their supporters toured the country drumming up support for the recruitment campaign 'and handed the white feather to every young man they encountered wearing civilian dress'.[42] The WSPU was renamed the Women's Party and now demanded compulsory national service for women. (Conscription for men was not introduced until 1916!) Even when, in 1916, Asquith was finally forced to concede the principle of full adult suffrage (to be introduced after the war), the super-patriotic Women's Party actually opposed such a suggestion on the grounds that the most pressing priority was to enfranchise the men in the fighting forces. In a remarkable reversal, the erstwhile militant supporters of women's suffrage campaigned ardently against this very issue, denouncing it as a ploy whereby Asquith was now, in Mrs Pankhurst's term, 'using the women to dish the men'.[43] The only consistency in their approach was their continued opposition to Asquith, whose days as Prime Minister were numbered.[44] In 1915, *The Suffragette*, now renamed *Britannia*, outdid almost every other chauvinist newspaper and periodical in its fervent (almost maniacal) support for a 'war of attrition'. Sylvia records that *Britannia*'s ardency, which entailed frequent criticism of government policy as too mild, led, on occasion, to suppression by the authorities.[45] To *Britannia*, the first Russian revolution of 1917 was a potential disaster. It was the occasion for Mrs Pankhurst to travel to Russia and plead with the new Kerensky government to honour the Tsarist commitment to the Triple Entente (Britain, France and Russia) and remain in the war. Kerensky did not need persuading, but the Russian people did. The second (Bolshevik) revolution of 1917 was, for Mrs Pankhurst and Christabel, a total abomination. It resulted in immediate Russian withdrawal and a separate peace treaty (Brest Litovsk), whereupon Mrs Pankhurst advocated armed intervention in Russia to defeat the Bolsheviks.[46]

In short, Sylvia's mother and sister had moved steadily and irrevocably to the right. Their early political allegiance to the ILP was almost impossible to imagine in the wake of their subsequent betrayal of all they had once supported. This political shift had, in the war years, also resulted in their jettisoning of the cause of women. The rift within the Pankhurst family was unhealable. Sylvia records that she wept when she heard of the pro-war stance taken by her mother and elder sister. The political rift also affected her younger sister, Adela, who, like Sylvia, was also anti-war, a socialist and a suffrage activist, but who was pursuing these activities in Australia. Their two brothers, Frank and Harry, were dead. Within the family, Sylvia had thus to stand alone.

The War and the Labour Movement

It would be incorrect to suppose that the older Pankhursts reflected the spirit of the times. Rather they were moving against it in view of the fact that the war years witnessed an acceleration in working-class militancy led by a unique rank-and-file movement which assumed a position of *de facto* leadership in the wake of the incorporation of the official leadership of the labour movement. War disrupts society. This was no exception, but far from disrupting the existing trends within the labour movement, it had the effect of concretising them. The militancy of labour's rank and file, as evidenced during the period 1910–14, continued unabated, whilst the exigencies of war gave labour's leaders the chance to become fully enmeshed within the state apparatus. The gulf between the leadership and the rank and file widened to such an extent that it was difficult for both to co-exist within the same organisations. The 'unofficial' opposition, reflecting the chasm between leaders and led, generated its own structures in the form of the shop stewards' movement and workers' committees. This, together with the heightened struggle for Irish independence (reaching a climax in the Easter Rising of 1916), and the later impact of the Russian revolution, lent this period a particularly militant character nationally and internationally. Sylvia was swept up in this tide, which continued after the war. In this sense she could claim with some justification that she was continuing the family tradition in contrast to other people 'who have forgotten their history'.[47]

This is not to underestimate the seduction of the pro-war lobby. British labour leaders maintained an anti-war stance up until the point, on 4 August 1914, that the government finally declared war on Germany. Thereafter, their opposition transformed itself not just into support, but to wholesale cooperation in the war effort. By the end of August the Labour Party and the TUC declared an 'industrial truce' for the duration of the war and lent their support to an all-party recruitment campaign. The British Socialist Party, led by Hyndman, supported this position until the Party leaders were defeated in 1915–16 by a rank-and-file revolt, and Hyndman himself was removed in 1916. On a primarily ethical basis, the ILP maintained an anti-war policy from the start, even though some of its leading parliamentary members did not. (As an ILP member, Ramsay MacDonald surprised his detractors by opposing the war. In consequence he resigned as leader of the Labour Party. His place was taken by Arthur Henderson.) Labour compliance was more than welcomed by a government faced with the problems of wartime production and the mass mobilisation of fighting men. As it became clear that the war would not be over by Christmas, the government became more dependent on a compliant labour leadership to act as their conduit to the masses. In order to achieve its wartime aims, it was clearly desirable for the state to operate through a process of consent rather than coercion, even if this meant, from the viewpoint of the leaders of organised labour, a hitherto unimagined degree of status in the machinery of government.

Not that coercion was far below the surface as the draconian measures adopted in 1915 showed. Apart from the Defence of the Realm Act, under which the government assumed the right to commandeer any factory and its workers it deemed necessary for war work, the Treasury Agreements and the Munitions of War Act were both concluded with explicit Labour and/or trade union support (by May 1915 there were three Labour MPs in the Coalition government, one of them, Arthur Henderson, in the cabinet). The two Treasury Agreements signed by government and trade union representatives confirmed labour's promise to abandon strike action for the duration of the war. It also drew the unions (including the Amalgamated Society of Engineers, whose members were principally affected) into agreeing to suspend 'restrictive practices' in skilled trades by agreeing to the use of unskilled or semi-skilled labour (particularly that of women) in the war industries at reduced rates of pay. This was known as 'dilution', and the credit for its invention was claimed by none other than Millicent Fawcett of the NUWSS.[48] To press home their advantage, the government rushed through the Munitions of War Act which made these agreements legally binding, extended their coverage to other industries and introduced the infamous 'leaving certificates'. This was a device whereby a worker could obtain other employment only on production of such a certificate and was clearly aimed at preventing sacked militants from working again. Promises that the government, in return for these massive concessions, would take steps to clamp down on the enhanced opportunities for profiteering, were seen as a fair *quid pro quo* by the labour leadership, although in practice this turned out to be quite meaningless.

Thus opened, in Lloyd George's phrase, 'a great new chapter in the history of Labour in its relations with the State'. Many pro-war women thought that this analysis could be applied to them. In a way Lloyd George was correct. As a result of the war, the Labour party was transformed from a pressure group struggling to gain a foothold in consensus politics, into being partially incorporated in the state machine. The incorporation was partial in the sense that, although the ambition of the leadership was flattered by the role they were now asked to play, that role was a very limited one. They were never real insiders in that they had no effect whatsoever on the formulation of policy, they were tolerated as useful brokers in the execution of policies decided by those who really held power. Pro-war women were similarly incorporated, although it would be a mistake to assume that they were rewarded for their pains.

The War, the Women's Movement and the ELFS

Just as the war generated a fissure in the already fragile unity of the labour movement, it played the same role in the women's movement. The WSPU Pankhursts were in the extreme wing of the pro-war lobby, but other suffrage organisations were similarly affected. The NUWSS was engulfed by war chauvinism. Its journal, *Common Cause*, declared that due to 'this great national crisis' the NUWSS has 'suspended their political activities' in order to conduct relief work since this was the best way 'to preserve the life of the race for the future ... the suffragists demand is for duties rather than for rights'.[49] The NUWSS thus turned itself into a 'Women's Active Service Corps' to assist in mobilising the nation for war work and for the relief of distress. A small group of seceders from the NUWSS formed the British section of the Women's International League.

At one level, the war work of the ELFS was similarly motivated by the desire to relieve distress. Indeed, it consumed much of its effort and attention during the first three years of the war. Two communal 'cost-price' restaurants were opened, a toy factory, a day nursery and mother and baby clinics flourished successfully, the latter in a former pub once known as 'The Gunmakers' Arms' and renamed 'The Mothers' Arms' by the ELFS. All the facilities enjoyed widespread local support and attracted admiration from outsiders. A journalist from the *Herald*, reporting on a visit to 400 Old Ford Road (the headquarters of the ELFS), was greatly impressed with what he saw and noted with approval 'that it is not the dispensing kind of charity' which characterised the ELFS' relief work, rather 'the feeling of independence is encouraged'.[50] Sylvia's book, *The Home Front*, gives a meticulous description of these activities all of which were designed to alleviate the crushing poverty of East-End women whose situation was made worse by the war and the removal of the male wage from the household. Although jobs for women increased, they were no compensation for the loss of income, especially since women were paid far less than the male rate anyway. Sylvia described the situation to a journalist:

> Acute distress has come suddenly to people who in normal times can just keep going and maintain appearances. The rise in prices has simply wiped out the very narrow margin which separates the weekly budget of most of the families down here from the starvation level ... Every day I find cases in which women and girls have had no food at all for two or three days.'[51]

Had the ELFS only concentrated on this kind of self-help to relieve distress it would not have distinguished itself from other women's organisations who were similarly attempting to plug the yawning chasm in social provision unfilled by the state. Indeed, as a social welfare organisation it earned great admiration from previously hostile sources which, like the *Evening Times*, chose to interpret the work of the ELFS as supportive of the nation. This paper was rarely pro-suffrage and very anti-socialist, yet it reported:

> Once again the suffragettes are showing that whatever may be their faults in other directions they are organisers of rare genius. These powers of organisation, which in the past, have been chiefly engaged in terrorising the nation, are now being

devoted to a very splendid and patriotic aim. Down in East London, where the slightest cog in the economic machine means acute misery ... the whole energies of the suffragettes' splendid organisation are being bent towards relieving the distress.[52]

However, there were two ways in which the work of the ELFS was distinctive. The first was that, unlike other groups, its social work was not predicated upon support for the war effort, and the second was that such work was not its sole preoccupation. In fact, as the war ground on, this kind of work became secondary to the ELFS' overtly political and eventually, as it saw it, revolutionary role. Walter Holmes, later a journalist working for the *Daily Worker*, who worked in a chemical factory in the East End from 1912 onwards, described Sylvia's work in these years thus:

what she aroused in the East End was a mass movement. Not only an enthusiatic following of young working-class women joined in her franchise campaign ... young workers came with them ... They filled the streets with their marching. The *Red Flag* and *The Internationale* resounded under the dim lights of 1914–15 ... Sylvia Pankhurst contributed a powerful opposition to the imperialist war.'[53]

From the very outset Sylvia resolutely opposed the war and although she never wavered in this, it took until 1915 to get the ELFS to share this view fully and openly. A special committee meeting was called 'to consider what we should do now that war has been declared',[54] at which Sylvia posed three alternatives: to go on as if nothing had happened; to make things better for those who were suffering because of the war; to make political capital out of the situation. The second was the preferred option, although by implication this entailed the third option as well. In deference to the sensibilities of ELFS members[55] it was thought that not much could be said directly about the war since so many people had relatives involved 'that they will not listen yet'.[56] Hackney members of the ELFS explicitly criticised Sylvia in June 1915 for her decision to organise a counter-demonstration to the WSPU procession which was called to demand compulsory military service. Sylvia defended herself and said that 'if they [the Hackney women] felt so aggrieved they should pass a vote of no confidence in her and she would resign'.[57] Clearly she had to tread very carefully. There is no question as to Sylvia's anti-war position, but she showed a deal of sensitivity in the way she propounded this view, because, as she later wrote, she 'felt sorrow in having to tell the relatives of soldiers that the war was in vain'.[58] Hence it was decided to concentrate on the issues of food supply and food prices and the relief of distress as well as the vote. Furthermore it was decided that ELFS members should serve on local distress committees, with the argument that such members should make 'the fullest possible use of this opportunity to help our East London neighbours especially the women and children at this time of national crisis. Such opportunities of doing important administrative work are seldom open to working women.'[59]

Equal Pay

The question of equal pay was seen as a vital adjunct of the relief of poverty and distress. Again the campaign launched by the ELFS on this further distinguished their conception of the true meaning of relief work and highlighted their stated aim of politicising such work in the long-term interests of women. An interesting correspondence between Lloyd George and Sylvia developed on this issue of equal pay. In answer to her demand that women receive equal pay for equal work, Lloyd George was reluctantly forced to concede that women would receive the same pay as men if they 'turn out the same quantity of work'.[60] At a conference held at the Board of Trade in April 1915, the government announced that this principle applied to piece-work rates but not to time work. Clearly the government was desperate to recruit women to war work – a view shared by the overwhelming majority of the predominantly middle-class conference audience, the tenor of which was represented by Eleanor Rathbone. She expressed her disgust at the poor response from women to the appeal of the government. Sylvia and Mrs Drake represented the ELFS at the conference and were apparently the only ones present who were in touch with the lives of working-class women.They were quick to exploit the contradiction in the state's need for women's labour, especially in armaments manufacture, and their refusal to pay them a living wage. Hence from April 1915 onward the ELFS launched a vigorous campaign on women's pay as well as exposing the horrors of the sweated trades, first publicly exposed to middle-class gaze at the *Daily News* sponsored exhibition of 1906 where, at the Queen's Hall in Regent Street, London, a visual display of women homeworkers in 45 of the grossly underpaid 'sweated trades' was exhibited for six weeks. This contained stalls which showed women carding buttons, sewing tennis balls, making matchboxes, sewing sacks, folding bibles, making artificial flowers, coffin tassles, slippers, umbrellas and much else. Sylvia and her group organised a similar exhibition in May 1915 at Caxton Hall, London, to expose the evil of 'sweating' on army contracts. The ELFS must be credited for being the main organisation campaigning on women's pay, and certainly the only one to launch the demand 'that the principle of equal pay for work of equal value shall be established throughout the entire field of industry'.[61] The policy was carried into the broader movement through the Labour War Emergency Council.[62] All sections of the labour and socialist movement were entitled to be represented on this Council, which was formed when war was declared. Its aim was to protect the interests of workers in the face of the inevitable economic dislocation which war would cause. The ELFS, represented by their two delegates, Sylvia and Mrs Parsons, must have caused quite a stir at the 1915 conference of the Labour War Emergency Council. They proposed a raft of amendments to otherwise fairly tame resolutions. All these concerned issues that the ELFS regarded as important for women workers and indicate, by the standards of the day, an 'advanced' feminist position: male unions were urged to admit women members; women's pay should be the same as that of men and their wages should never fall below that of the unskilled male rate; maintenance grants of no less than £1 per week to be paid to all women on government training schemes. Finally, the ELFS demanded 'that the long overdue reform of universal suffrage will be placed on the statute book'.[63]

Feminist resolutions were followed up by a flurry of public activity during July and August 1915. A 'Procession to Parliament' was organised on 12 July with the slogans of 'Equal Pay for Men and Women', 'Down with Sweating' and 'Votes for Women'. In August a joint demonstration with similar demands was held. The significance of this event was in the breadth of labour-movement support it attracted. In addition to the ELFS, it was sponsored by the United Suffragists, the Herald League, the BSP, some ILP branches, and several trade unions including the Dockers' Union, the Engineers' Union, the

Electrical Union and the National Union of Railwaymen. The same bodies organised a second demonstration in September 1915 with a mass rally at Trafalgar Square. It was here that the news of Keir Hardie's death was announced – a great personal loss to Sylvia. In an long article memorialising him, she stated simply that 'James Keir Hardie has been the greatest human being of our time'.[64] His death induced Sylvia, according to her own account,[65] to question the wisdom of her campaign to ameliorate conditions during the war rather than devote all her attention, as Hardie had done, to opposing the war altogether.

Votes for Women

Throughout the war the ELFS distinguished itself in maintaining its commitment to its original purpose – the fight for women's suffrage. Given the vast array of other activities in which it was involved it would have been easy to lose sight of this. In January 1916 a report of the work of the ELFS during 1915 was published in the *Woman's Dreadnought* – it was an impressive record. Each of the by then seven branches had held two indoor meetings weekly. Seventy public meetings were held in all in addition to three Trafalgar Square demonstrations and the May Day Rally in Victoria Park.

Despite this remarkable activism Sylvia warned against complacency, arguing that 'when organisations grow to a certain size they are liable to develop cliques, and the old members, forgetting to realize the need for perpetual growth, sometimes imagine that things must go on as they always have.'[66] It is difficult to understand precisely the meaning of such coded language. Certainly there had been internal dissention within the organisation since mid-1915, and some members and paid organisers had resigned,[67] but there is no discernible political disagreement which might explain this. It may be that a new campaign on suffrage – the demand for human suffrage – advocated by the ELFS in January 1916, was seen by Sylvia as a way out of internal local squabbles. Whatever the reason, the issue of human suffrage now emerged as an important campaigning demand, attracting support from the labour left. It had profound repercussions on the ELFS in that it changed its orientation away from being a predominantly women's suffrage organisation. Although the ELFS had never concentrated exclusively on women's suffrage, the very fact that it retained the word 'suffragette' in its title was a clear indication of its antecedents and current orientation. When, in 1916, Asquith announced that his government would introduce full adult suffrage after the war, it was clear that campaigning on women's suffrage alone was inappropriate. Sylvia wrote a long article for the *Woman's Dreadnought* entitled 'Why Wait?',[68] in which she analysed the history of the women's suffrage movement and criticised its failure to demand votes for all women. She then went on to raise the demand for human suffrage and anticipated the feminist counter-arguments which might be used against this. Why should women help more men get the vote when men are already in a powerful position? Will not this result in women being used as campaign fodder once again? Her answer to this was that such a possibility was highly unlikely given the strength of the women's movement in Britain; international examples showed that women got the vote only when property qualifications for men had been abolished.

Clearly in the circumstances of 1916, when a full commitment to adult suffrage had been announced by the government, this change in the policy of the ELFS was entirely understandable. However, it has attracted surprisingly little comment given the obvious implications it had for the future of the organisation and the bitter controversy in the past within the women's movement and betweeen the women's movement and the labour movement on the issue of adult suffrage. Certainly it represented a logical progression for Sylvia who, as we have seen, had for a long time been uncomfortable with the traditional women-only suffrage demand. Now, in the Britain of 1916, all the champions of the traditional demand had deserted the cause entirely, leaving the way clear for a revival of the adultist position, only this time no one could suspect this was a ploy to 'sell out' women. Human suffrage meant what it said, and, more importantly, those who advocated it were fully committed to its meaning.

4

Feminism and Socialism

The experience of the war together with Sylvia's long-standing commitment to the working class and the labour movement had, as we have seen, resulted in a steady shift to the left of what was formerly the ELFS. Having changed its name in 1916 to the Workers' Suffrage Federation, it renamed itself again in 1918 as the Workers' Socialist Federation (WSF). Similarly, the title of the paper was changed in 1917 from the *Woman's Dreadnought* to the *Workers' Dreadnought*. This reflected the revolutionary spirit in the rank and file of the labour movement as expressed in the steady growth and influence of shop stewards' and workers' committees, but above all else it reflected the profound impact of the Russian revolution.

By June 1917, a report of the annual conference of the WSF announced that one of its chief tasks was to work for the abolition of capitalism 'and for the establishment of a socialist commonwealth in which the means of production and distribution shall be deployed in the interests of the people'.[1] The *Workers' Dreadnought* was almost completely devoted to publicising and propagandising the socialist cause. Its tone and content were markedly different from that of previous years. It contained many articles of a theoretical Marxist nature written by the leading socialists of the day, as well as regular reports of labour movement activity both at home and abroad. A sense of urgency and dynamism pervaded the columns of the paper which increasingly reflected the heady, revolutionary spirit of the times. With a circulation of around 10,000, the *Workers' Dreadnought* can be regarded as one of the most important anti-war, non-sectarian socialist papers in Britain, achieving an influential position by opening its columns to all shades of opinion on the left. Its role in this respect has been underestimated by labour movement historians, but clearly it was recognised at the time, which may account for the fact that Siegfried Sassoon (later to achieve fame alongside Wilfred Owen and Robert Graves as an anti-war poet and author) chose it as the vehicle for his now famous statement 'Finished with the war: a soldier's declaration'. This explosive anti-war declaration by a serving officer who had won the Military Cross for bravery was published as a letter in the *Dreadnought*[2] before it was published elsewhere and raised in the House of Commons (on 4 August 1917), by which time the military authorities had safely detonated its effect by certifying Sassoon as mentally ill.[3] Sylvia had already shown great courage in printing soldiers' letters from the front exposing the horrors of the war, but the publication of Sassoon's declaration, the opening sentence of which stated clearly that he was writing 'as an act of wilful defiance of military authority', placed the paper and its editor in greater danger than the author.[4] The editorial in the issue containing Sassoon's declaration was deemed by the authorities to have incited paralysis of the war effort and hence the offices of the *Dreadnought* were raided.

The paper was under constant government surveillance not only for its 'treasonable' anti-war stance, which had become more forceful since the anti-conscription campaign of 1916. Its revolutionary tone and message alarmed the government even more. In 1917 two issues were suppressed. The government invoked Sections 51 and 52 of the Defence of the Realm Act to prevent the Blackfriars Press from printing one of the October issues. The Council of the Workers' Suffrage Federation decided to go ahead anyway and print it in pamphlet form[5] and the 10 November issue was suppressed altogether following another government raid. Such interference did little to tone down the content and message of the paper, which continued to publicise anti-war and labour movement activity at home and abroad. John McLean, the leading Scottish Marxist, frequently wrote for the paper. As an interesting aside from the hurly-burly of the struggle, the paper printed a major article by McLean entitled 'Independent working-class education',[6] in which he asserted that the government was so alarmed by the popularity of the revolutionary socialist message which was being propagated via thousands of workers' education classes, discussion groups and popular pamphlets, that it intended to make use of the Workers' Education Association (WEA) as an antidote to Marxism. McLean himself played a major role as a populariser of Marxism, as did the *Dreadnought* itself, albeit in a more eclectic fashion and despite the fact that Sylvia was not and would not claim to be a Marxist theoretician.

T. Walton Newbold, who was later (in 1922) to be elected as the communist MP for Motherwell, wrote a long series over several issues on 'Capitalism and the counter revolution'. The Italian anarcho-socialist Silvio Corio (later to be Sylvia's partner and father of her son, Richard[7]) wrote a series of historical articles about Karl Marx. Margaret Watt wrote a major article on the importance of 'scientific socialism'.[8] Translations of speeches and articles by Lenin were printed regularly, as were reports and analyses of the Russian revolution, many of them written by the American socialist, John Reed, in a series entitled 'Red Russia'.[9] Internationalism was a prominent feature of the paper. It contained accounts and analyses of the revolutionary struggle and labour movement activity in Ireland, Greece, Italy, Bulgaria, Austria-Hungary and especially Germany. Germany had, for many years, the largest socialist movement of any country in Europe and, although like many others, it had split over its attitude to the war, the forces of the left were strong enough to launch a socialist revolution in 1919. However, at least a year before this the paper was carrying articles about the spread of strike activity in Germany and was predicting the likelihood of a political confrontation with the state.[10] Such internationalism was not confined to Europe. Sylvia showed an early awareness, unusual even among the left, of the importance of the anti-colonial struggle, especially in India.[11] The paper was noted too for its strong support of the Irish national struggle against centuries of British rule. The Easter Rising of 1916 was fully and sympathetically reported, as were the subsequent events in the Irish liberation struggle. Indeed, the paper's reporting of the Irish rising was a scoop. It was a first hand, on-the-spot account written by a WSF member, Patricia Lynch.[12] Sylvia was deeply saddened by the British army's execution of the Irish leaders, in particular James Connolly, whom she admired greatly and regarded as a friend.

The Russian revolution had given an enormous boost to the class struggle in Britain. Given that very few members of the WSF were actively involved in the shop stewards' and workers' committee movement which had spread rapidly in industrial centres during the war, it is a credit to Sylvia's political class consciousness that she saw the importance of such a movement and gave it coverage in the paper. Thus it was that the paper reported regularly on industrial disputes and trade union activity. W. F. Watson of the Amalgamated Society of Engineers[13] wrote a weekly column entitled 'Workshop notes'. Apparently Watson himself suggested the idea to Sylvia and had wanted a regular centre-page slot. He assured her that the inclusion of his column would increase the paper's circulation. By April 1918 it was reported that Watson's notes had been responsible for a circulation increase of 3,000 copies.[14] None the less, he was still denied the centre pages. Other trade union activists, like J. T. Murphy,[15] the leader of the Sheffield Workers' Committee, and Harry Pollitt (a boilermaker, later to become general secretary of the Communist Party of Great Britain), also wrote for the paper on industrial issues.

Apart from its refreshing lack of sectarianism, it could be said of the *Dreadnought* that in its commitment to the class struggle and revolutionary politics at home and abroad it differed little from the many other socialist papers and broadsheets extant at the time. However, there were two distinguishing features of the paper which make it stand out from the rest – features which were and remained the abiding hallmark of Sylvia's politics throughout her adult life. One, of course, was the long-standing commitment to women's rights, which had been the starting point of her political activism in the East End. The other was much more unusual for the time – an understanding of imperialism and its association with the poisonous ideology of racism.[16] To these two must be added something more intangible, but no less important – the freshness and readability of the paper. It was well designed and laid out with effective use of illustrations, cartoons and pictures.

Women's Suffrage

Sylvia's feminism underwent a profound change from 1917 onwards. Was feminist politics the inevitable casualty of her greater commitment to class politics and revolutionary activism? In one sense this was indeed the case – the very fact that her organisation changed its name to the Workers' Suffrage Federation (later the Workers' Socialist Federation) and that the *Woman's Dreadnought* was renamed the *Workers' Dreadnought* is an indication of broader priorities. But this in itself did not betoken any less of a commitment to the women's cause. In essence, the change meant that what had begun as a single-issue campaign for women's suffrage was now located firmly in the struggle to end exploitation not only for working-class women, but for all workers. In other words, Sylvia had adopted, albeit unsystematically, a Marxist analysis which postulated that the root of women's oppression lay within the capitalist mode of production which, through its extraction of surplus value, exploited all workers. Women's oppression could thus only be ended with the end of class exploitation and this could only be achieved through a revolutionary overthrow of the capitalist system itself and the state which supported it. This was the (unspoken) ideological justification for Sylvia's preoccupation with the broader revolutionary stage and although this in itself did not make her any less of a feminist, it had a great impact on her stance on the suffrage question.

Mention has already been made (Chapter 3) of the move to the demand for human suffrage early in 1917. This was concretised in one of the resolutions passed by the annual conference of the WSF in May 1917 which declared its opposition to the Speaker's conference report on electoral reform.[17] The WSF stated that no measure was acceptable unless it provided for complete adult suffrage and that the WSF would only cooperate with those organisations sharing a similar aim. This precipitated a stormy debate in the National Council for Adult Suffrage to which Sylvia's Joint Demonstration Committee[18] was affiliated. The government's Franchise Bill, introduced in 1917, was, of course, unacceptable to the WSF and to all socialists since although, for the first time, women were included in its provisions, it none the less proposed to enfranchise only women over 30 on the basis of a small property qualification. It was a shabby all-party compromise which explicitly rejected the principle of equal suffrage in favour of the safer bet of enfranchising older women on the presumption that they were likely to be wives and mothers. This, of course, was a strange reversal of the nineteenth-century constitutionalists' suffrage demand which sought to exclude married women on the grounds that women lost the right to an independent role on wedlock. It would thus appear to demolish the oft-repeated argument that women gained the vote as a reward for their war work since it was younger, single women who were the most directly active in this regard, as workers in munitions factories or as nurses in the Voluntary Aid Detachments (VADs). Such women were explicitly excluded.

Sylvia was almost the only feminist voice in opposition to the Franchise Bill. However, its anti-egalitarianism was not the only reason for her antipathy towards it. She saw that the government's motive was to take the sting out of any further agitation on the question by leaving it 'in the hands of the ladies he [Asquith] had seen'[19] – that is the 'well-dressed' women of the 'respectable' suffrage societies. There is some credence in this argument, especially in view of the fact that the 'well-dressed' element had, during the war, according to Martin Pugh, contributed to 're-awakening conventional notions about the separate spheres', and this 'in spite of, or even because of the unusual wartime roles performed by women'.[20] The behaviour of politicians, supported since 1914 by women like Mrs Pankhurst, served to confirm the traditional view that women's role was in the family – a role which had been interrupted by the exigencies of war. This was the safe bedrock on which the 'land fit for heroes' was to be built. But there was an additional reason for Sylvia's antipathy to the Bill which is to be found in her changed attitude to the parliamentary process itself. It was not simply that the WSF was now firmly committed to adult suffrage on a democratic basis. The WSF's May 1917 conference also supported 'the recall and election of ministers and judges by referendum vote'.[21] Such a demand, a moderate foretaste of things to come, clearly distanced the WSF from the main suffrage organisations and it was from this time onwards excluded from them. The WSF was not unduly bothered by this and resolved 'that we go on as before … trusting no society but ourselves'.[22] Notwithstanding this, the WSF continued to campaign for 'human suffrage', a position symbolised by the change in name from the ELFS in 1916 and the change in name of the paper in 1917. Sylvia, together with George Lansbury, the BSP and some trade unionists, set up the Adult Suffrage Joint Committee, but beyond passing resolutions it conducted little in the way of mass activity. Clearly the days of mass campaigning for women's suffrage were now at an end.

From this time onward there is little mention of the suffrage question in the *Dreadnought* or in the minutes of the WSF, despite the fact that the Bill enfranchising women over the age of 30 gained Royal Assent in February 1918. For Sylvia this was not a great victory for women and not a matter for rejoicing. She pointed out that 'less than half the women will get the vote by the new Act … the new Act does not remove the sex disability; it does not establish equal suffrage'.[23] However, even if the franchise had been granted in full measure 'it could not seem to us as a great joy-giving boon in these sad days' given the awful horrors of the war. Later in the year little coverage was accorded to the first general election in which women could participate. Seventeen women stood as candidates, one of whom was Sylvia's sister Christabel, who stood for her newly formed and very short-lived Women's Party.[24] Only four women stood as

Labour candidates, none as Conservatives.[25] The remainder, who stood as Independents and Liberals, were certainly not progressive, with the exception of the revolutionary Sinn Fein candidate who had fought in the 1916 Easter Rising, Countess Constance Markiewicz. She was the only woman to be elected in 1918, although she refused to take her seat as a protest against British rule in Ireland. Certainly the election was a great disappointment for women, especially for radical suffragists, since the Labour Party, which had seemed such a hopeful prospect before the war, had adopted such a small number of women candidates. But this fact alone does not account for the WSF's lack of attention to the election. The explanation for this curious silence, which stands in such sharp contrast to the previous years of painstaking coverage and militant campaigning, is to be found in Sylvia's increased disillusionment with the parliamentary process. This was expressed in an important article she wrote entitled 'Parliament doomed'.[26] In it she advanced the view that parliament's decision to enfranchise women was made not, as was usually supposed, as a reward for war work, but was motivated by fear of Bolshevism. The women who enter parliament, she argued, whatever their politics, 'will go in and play the sad old party game that achieves so little' whereas those who remain outside, 'the more active and independent women', remain 'a discontented crowd of rebels'. These rebels were waiting for the Soviets to replace parliament, which, according to Sylvia, had now become an outdated nineteenth-century institution. She did not go as far as some (e.g. the Socialist Labour Party) in advocating a 'Don't Vote' position, but she expressed surprise when she learned that she had been mentioned as a possible parliamentary candidate for the Sheffield Hallam seat. She, of course, refused on the grounds that she was 'in accord with the policy of the WSF' which 'regards parliament as an out of date machine'.[27] In fact, her stance was very close to an abstentionist one. As we shall see, this hostility to parliament was later to become a major hallmark of her political position, isolating her from many other socialists during the discussions on the formation of the Communist Party. For the moment, however, her position isolated her from the mainstream of the women's movement and the labour movement, both of which enthusiastically participated in the extension of the franchise, despite the fact that there were criticisms and reservations about the terms of the act.

Thus the *Dreadnought* barely mentioned the 1918 election. Instead it devoted space to what it clearly regarded as more important world events – the Versailles Peace Conference and the progress of socialism in Soviet Russia. In 1923, the second election in which women could vote and be candidates saw the return of eight women MPs. This was not ignored – it occasioned a more reflexive and analytical approach from Sylvia[28] who acknowledged the prejudice women had to overcome from the party machines. However, she argued, it was precisely because women are the prisoners of their political parties that they would remain ineffective. Even on questions relating to women, women MPs would not necessarily prove their worth, they 'may sometimes show themselves a trifle before or a trifle behind the general standard of their party by adhering in some respects to what has come to be generally regarded as the accepted programme of feminism'.[29] However, in an interesting comment on the very women's movement to which she had devoted all her early adult life, she went on to say that this feminist programme was only regarded as acceptable because 'it was adopted by certain women of the middle and upper classes, who were, for their day more or less advanced though narrow and prejudiced in many respects' and who, whilst 'forceful and energetic' enough to build a women's movement, did so primarily in order to further their own class interests. Their 'programme is in many respects, retrograde and, in all respects incompatible with socialism'.[30] Clearly she had her mother and sister in mind in writing this, but as a judgement of the women's movement, it is, none the less, surprising that she threw out the suffrage baby with the middle-class bath water. In the same article she continued the 'parliament doomed' refrain and judged that there was little difference between male and female politicians: neither are desirable and 'the less the world has of either the better'.

Post-Suffrage: Feminism in the Inter-war Years

Even allowing for Sylvia's growing distaste for 'the sad old party game', it is still hard to account for the lack of attention to the vast array of problems faced by working-class women in the immediate post-war period. A report on *The Position of Women*

After the War issued in 1917 by the Standing Joint Committee of
Industrial Women's Organisations[31] feared that the end of the
war would reverse the gains made by women workers. It noted
that the war had brought about 'two great changes in the position of women workers, both of which have been to their
advantage'. One was that many new, better-paid trades were
open to them and the second was that trade union action had
secured wage rises in 'women's trades'. The report concluded
that 'every advantage should be taken of the present situation
to secure a far higher standard of life for women, and a position
of general industrial equality with men' and that this could be
achieved by securing 'the principle of equal pay for equal work'.
The WSF supported this principle, although it would not have
supported other aspects of the report, in particular its ambivalence on the question of married mothers' right to work. None
the less, at this stage, campaigning work among women solely,
on this or any other issue, was less of a priority for Sylvia. By
1917 it was clear that the WSF was abandoning its schemes for
relieving distress which had characterised its wartime activity to
date. In October 1917 it was reported to the WSF Council that
the Bow restaurant was affected by dissension among the staff
and that the Poplar restaurant was failing and should be 'given
up'. The Toy Factory was now an independent organisation and
the Council, accepting this, wanted it to be run on the lines of
a workers' cooperative managed by a factory committee 'on
which outside people may be elected but only those who hold
socialist and co-operative views'.[32] There is little further
mention of these organisations or of this type of activity by and
among working-class women. The Bow restaurant was closed in
April 1918. Another name change for the WSF was contem-
plated, although not adopted, in December 1918. Sylvia
favoured the title Workers' Communist Federation ('since this is
the name chosen by the Bolsheviki of Russia'[33]), and pledged to
establish the dictatorship of the proletariat. Clearly, running
cost-price restaurants and other such 'palliative' measures had
no place in this grand revolutionary design, as she herself can-
didly acknowledged years later. In her autobiographical notes
she admitted that her support for the Russian revolution had an
adverse impact on East-End welfare schemes and that as result
she 'lost friends and co-workers'.[34]

   To some extent Sylvia's coolness to the 1918 suffrage
measure was justified since, as we have seen, the election in that
year did little to fulfil the pre-war hopes of women. The revival

of the women's movement after the war similarly offered little to women who had been radicalised by the militancy of the labour movement during the war. Compared with the pre-war years, it was a feminism of a very different type. The unifying bond of the suffrage campaign now gave way to competing trends within the women's movement. Radical suffragists in the NUWSS, like Selina Cooper and Ada Neild Chew, who had sought to establish a link between socialism and feminism now found that such a project was more difficult than ever. As Jill Liddington notes, 'The dovetailing of the socialism and feminism of the immediate pre-war years now seemed almost impossible'.[35] The NUWSS was renamed the National Union of Societies for Equal Citizenship (NUSEC), and in 1919 Eleanor Rathbone replaced Millicent Fawcett as its president. Rathbone championed the 'new feminism' as expressed in the objective of the NUSEC which was to 'obtain all other reforms, economic, legislative and social as are necessary to secure a real equality of liberties, status and opportunities between men and women'.[36] Radical suffragists like Selina Cooper found a temporary home in this organisation. Sylvia, however, was not involved in the 'new feminism' of the 1920s. Unlike the radical suffragists she had already broken with labourism and with the mainstream suffrage movement. By now her major preoccupation was with the revolutionary shop stewards' committees and the development of the communist movement (see Chapter 5). Despite the rediscovery of some of the positive aspects of the 'new feminism'[37] it is clear that working-class women were largely uninvolved in its organisational work. That is not to say that their interests were ignored, but rather that they were subjects of what was primarily a middle-class movement which adopted pressure group-style lobbying work. There was little in the way of the mass campaigning and mobilisation which had characterised the suffrage struggle. A multiplicity of causes emerged, the chief amongst them being birth control, family allowances and equal pay. However, the ideological basis of these demands fell far short of any socialist theoretical perspective. Rathbone, as the leading ideological light of the 'new feminism', saw all three issues as linked. She advocated the payment of family allowances (or family endowment as she termed it) in order both to assist the eradication of child poverty and to help raise women's low wages. Birth control, by reducing the size of working-class families, would also help to combat poverty. Women's role in the family lay at the centre of her concerns, as did the eugenic consideration that the 'national stock' must be improved and 'endowing motherhood' was the chief means of ensuring that 'the less fit elements' in society could be assisted to combat the degeneration of the British race. Her pioneering work in campaigning for family allowances, whilst in itself a progressive aim and which was ultimately fulfilled in 1945, was pursued for reasons which were not quite as laudable as the outcome. In essence, Rathbone saw state provision of family allowances as the means by which the growing demand for equal pay for women could be circumvented. For her, equal pay was unlikely to be achieved and its effect would be 'to perpetuate and intensify the existing tendency of the two sexes to become segregated in different occupations and to give women even less equality of opportunity than they have at present'.[38]

The immediate and pressing needs of women workers after the war were not addressed by the NUSEC nor by the mainstream labour movement. The hopes of the Standing Joint Committee of Industrial Women's Organisations were dashed when, within a few months of peace, 600,000 women were made unemployed. Apart from domestic service there were few other jobs open to them and, to ensure that such women had no illusions about the temporary nature of their war-time substitution, the government rushed through the restoration of the Pre-War Practices Act in 1918.[39] This Act, welcomed by the trade union leaders, ensured that 'men's jobs' were restored to them. The major target of the 'normalisation' process was married women. A report of the Women's Employment Committee of the Ministry of Reconstruction asserted that 'the employment of married women outside their homes is not to be encouraged'.[40]

In short, the 'new feminism' and the leadership of the labour movement, whilst pressing for reforms, were unwilling in the post-war years to challenge the values of the capitalist system. This was in sharp contrast to the continued militancy of rank-and-file workers. 1919 witnessed the broadest and most serious strike wave yet seen. Thirty-five million working days were lost in strike action – six times as many as in the previous year. This included strikes of those normally relied upon to carry out the repressive functions of the state – the police and the armed forces. Miners, transport workers and printers joined those who had been taking action throughout the war. Their mood was influenced by the news of the workers' risings in Germany and Hungary and their strong support for the fledgling Soviet

Russia. At the forefront was the Clyde Workers' Committee which organised a mass strike in January 1919, accompanied by mass picketing, for the 40-hour week. Unlike the wartime strikes, this one was not defensive – it was a political offensive against the power of capital. It was all the stronger for its well-established links with discharged soldiers and sailors. (Even before the war ended these latter were organised in the Federation of Discharged Soldiers and Seamen.) Women too were fully involved in the action and on the picket lines. The huge demonstration in George Square, Glasgow, resulted in a battle with the forces of law and order, supported by young troops sent there by a panic-stricken government anxious to nip the 'Bolshevik spirit' in the bud. Strike leaders were arrested and Glasgow fell under virtual military occupation. In Belfast too a huge strike wave paralysed the city.

The *Dreadnought* fully reported these events and paid particular attention to the role of working women in them. The demand for equal pay inspired the 1918 strike of women bus workers in London, followed shortly after by women tube workers. So, although Sylvia had moved away from women-only politics, was unimpressed by the Women's Suffrage Act and was clearly disaffected from the tenor and ideological stance of the post-war women's movement, she retained a feminist perspective within what she regarded as the more fruitful terrain of revolutionary class politics. For her, feminism was not replaced by socialism – rather she regarded the latter as the only means of achieving full political and economic equality for women. It is also clear that she had a well-thought-out position, informed by Marxism, on the nature of women's oppression. Her views were ideologically opposed to the 'new feminists" underlying acceptance of the capitalist patriarchal basis of marriage and the family. She viewed marriage forms as 'characteristic of the society which produces them'[41] and hence that monogamous marriage was typical of societies based on private property. Marriage, she argued, had little to do with love but was induced by women's economic dependency on men since 'average wage standards do not usually permit a woman to bear and rear children by her own unassisted earnings'.[42] She was unafraid to state her own radical views on the question of sex and marriage:

> We believe that marriage should not be the subject of legal contract. We are for free sexual unions, contracted and ter-

minated at will ... We believe that loveless unions should not be maintained ... we desire parenthood to be based on mutual love and mutual intention.[43]

She practised what she preached. In 1927 she gave birth, out of wedlock, to her only child, Richard. She firmly believed in matriarchy, in 'motherhood without marriage' and in the socialisation of housework so that women could be 'emancipated from household tasks' and retain their own names, 'the preservation of the symbol of personality'.[44] She disputed the commonly held view that women were economically dependent on men and instead denounced the prevailing system in which men's 'comfort and earning capacity'[45] was dependent on women to clean, cook and sew for them. This situation, she argued, was exacerbated in mining communities, where the struggle to maintain cleanliness was particularly hard and hence women never had time for themselves, much less take part in socialist politics. She observed that 'the South Wales miners are probably the most highly organised body of workers in the world; their wives take a smaller part in the workers' movement than the women of many other districts'.[46]

Such attitudes were more redolent of the 'new woman' of the early years of the suffrage campaign than of the 'new feminism' of the inter-war period. However, Sylvia went beyond the anti-marriage views of, for example, her sister Christabel. The latter was opposed to marriage since she regarded men as the repositaries of venereal diseases[47] – a subject which came gradually to obsess her. Others like the early suffragist, Mona Caird,[48] saw marriage as the chief form of women's enslavement. But these 'new women' of the Mona Caird stamp, although rejecting the traditional role of women, paid little or no attention to the relationship between women's oppression and the wider society. Nor did they advance any views on how mothers with no private means of their own could survive. Theirs was a feminism born of individualism which meant that beyond campaigning for the vote they had no social programme which encompassed the needs of working-class women. The 'new feminists', however, took the needs of working-class women as their starting point, but in so doing constructed a social programme which would enable them to 'fit' more comfortably within their traditionally accepted sphere. This did not rule out the practicality of paid work outside the home, but apart from professional women, the generally accepted view was that such work should cease upon marriage. While Eleanor Rathbone did not accept the conventional view that men earned a 'family wage' large enough to keep their wives and children (and roundly attacked it as a fallacy), this did not, as we have seen, lead her in the direction of equal pay. Sylvia did not accept the theoretical underpinnings of the 'new feminist' family-centred approach. Instead of family allowances to relieve the poverty of working-class women, she advocated a 'progeny fund' into which all men, whether they were fathers or not, would pay a percentage of their income on 'the premise that all men are potential fathers of all children and consequently have to provide for them'.[49] She envisaged that the tax would be levied for one generation only and that thereafter the fund would be boosted by the addition of the property of childless men who died intestate. This idea of a progeny tax by avoiding 'taking the trouble of ascertaining each individual father or making him accountable by the device of marriage'[50] was in essence a device rendering marriage and the monogamous nuclear family obsolete. The system would not stop love relationships and within them women conceding, voluntarily, paternity rights, but this was not to be automatic, since Sylvia's over-riding concern was that centuries of women's subjugation should be replaced by matriarchy. Through such a matriarchal movement feminism would pass from its present defensive phase to an offensive one in which women would take their rights rather than ask for them. Her argument here is certainly very advanced and belies the notion that she was unconcerned with the position of women after the decline of the suffrage campaign. However, her argument is also confused, since in the same article she also poses another way of women achieving the same goal of financial independence by 'increasing the efficiency of the feminine sex' through women establishing 'a business of their own, even if only on a very small scale'. Such a project was very firmly rooted in the capitalist system upon which a form of non-state matriarchy could be based. Apparently she was offering a choice between compulsion in the form of the progeny tax or voluntarism in the form of women's entrepreneurial self-organisation through the stimulus of market forces. This latter argument was highly untypical of her thinking and finds little or no echo in any of her other writing.

Sylvia's experience of pregnancy and childbearing led her to publish, in 1930, *Save the Mothers*. Its lengthy subtitle, *A Plea for Measures to Prevent the Annual Loss of about 3000 Child Bearing*

Mothers and 20,000 Infant Lives in England and Wales and a Similar Grievous Wastage in other Countries[51], left no doubt as to its subject matter and purpose. In it she advocated such measures as a national maternity service, non-contributory maternity benefit, a home-help scheme, pre- and post-natal mother and infant clinics, extension of paid maternity insurance benefit to working mothers, children's allowances, and the raising of the school leaving age to 16. In its way this book had as much influence on the shaping of public policy as did Eleanor Rathbone's work on family allowances. Ramsay MacDonald, leader of the Labour Party and then Prime Minister of the second (minority) Labour government, welcomed her proposals and, in a rare commitment on a feminist issue, he as good as pledged that the Labour Party would take action along the lines that she suggested: 'A complete scheme must ensure for the mother fully qualified medical and nursing care. She must also be relieved of any household worry both by the provision of help in the home and by some financial help ... '.[52]

Maternity benefit was one of the means to alleviate the plight of working-class women, especially the unmarried ones, during pregnancy and childbirth, but Sylvia was aware that this was neither the root nor the answer to women's oppression. Although she had become disenchanted with communism by 1924 and joined the Labour Party in 1948, she retained a deep, although not always an active, commitment to women's liberation throughout her life. Her writings on women, mostly unpublished, indicate a continuing attachment to socialist feminism and a critical approach to the individualism of the 'new feminism'. She was deeply disappointed by the result of the franchise struggle. Reflecting upon it around 21 years after the death of Emily Wilding Davison[53] in an article on 'Women's citizenship', Sylvia declared that she was not satisfied with the state of the women's movement, the status of women and the general lack of social progress. The only sign of women's emancipation 'displays itself mainly in cigarettes and shorts' and the growth in the number of professional and business women whose 'aims are mainly narrowed to personal needs'. So much was expected of women's citizenship which the pioneers hoped 'would open a new era of world happiness and social wisdom'; instead, the 1930s were witnessing mass unemployment, economic stagnation and a drift to war. Women in parliament had made little difference, they 'have sponsored no epoch making causes'. What was needed was a rebirth of the women's movement, lit by the fire which stimulated pre-war women's militancy. Such a movement would tackle poverty, slum dwelling, inadequate education (which 'has made no great strides this century') and would mount an effective protest against the sacking of married women teachers and local authority workers. In 1935, during the general election campaign, she echoed the theme of the potential power of women, a majority of the electorate, which could be used to fight for peace and social reform 'if we combined in a party of our own'.[54]

Although she remained a feminist after the women's vote had been won, Sylvia did not belong to or form any women's organisation in these years which gave voice to such a feminist programme. She wrote a great deal during these years and was spurred into activism by the threat of fascism and war. Certainly she would not have found a comfortable home in the NUSEC, which anyway had declined by the end of the 1920s and was finally wound up in 1933. Although a plethora of other women's organisations existed, the Townwomen's Guild being perhaps the largest, Sylvia would not have found its politics appealing.

Clearly Sylvia's views on women were much too advanced for the tame and respectable feminism of the post-war years. In any case, her primary concern from 1917–24 lay not in the winning of piecemeal reform, but in overthrowing the capitalist system altogether. Rather than the NUSEC, she found a more 'comfortable' place in the Communist Party.

5

Communism

As we have seen, Sylvia and her organisation in its various incarnations had moved steadily to the left during the war. What had begun as a small but influential and effective women's suffrage organisation in the East End had transformed itself into an influential, albeit still small, revolutionary socialist party. By 1918 the WSF was open to men, although its leadership, unusually among left organisations, was still predominantly female. Its weekly paper, the *Workers' Dreadnought*, had an enviably high circulation of over 10,000 and was read throughout the country, although its main distribution was in London. The impact of national and international events continued to exercise a determining influence on the fortunes of the WSF and its leader. All political activists are influenced by the prevailing political climate. Some, of course, help to influence the climate, others merely reflect it. To some extent Sylvia did both.

For women, however, the issue is not quite so straightforward. Although women activists had come to prominence and made their mark as leaders during the suffrage campaign and in other women-only organisations (e.g. the Co-operative Women's Guild, the Women's Trade Union League and the National Federation of Women Workers), it was rare to find a woman in the leadership of a socialist organisation. Politics in Britain was still an exclusively male preserve. This applied to the groups on the left as well as to mainstream organisations. Although Sylvia, by 1918, had reduced her commitment to 'women's issues' in favour of the class struggle to achieve socialism, this did not mean that she jettisoned her feminism. Nor should her achievement as a woman in a male revolutionary world be understated. She had, since 1917, tirelessly championed the activities of the Russian Bolsheviks at a time when the full significance of the revolution was imperfectly appreciated. A West Indian revolutionary, Claude McKay, said of her that 'she was one of the first leaders in England to stand up for Soviet Russia'.[1] She fully accepted such a view of her own role in this respect. Despite her later disillusionment with the Soviet

Union and communism in general, she none the less continued
to regard her work in support of the revolution as pioneering.
In an unpublished letter she stated, 'I was one of the earliest and
most active supporters of the Bolshevists when they first came
into international prominence'.[2]

Apart from the constant stream of pro-revolution articles
appearing in the *Dreadnought*, it is clear that her activity from
1918 bears testimony to McKay's (and her own) observation. In
September 1918 she established the People's Russia Information
Bureau (PRIB). This was a broad-left organisation, the committee
of which consisted of representatives of affiliated organisations –
the London Workers' Committee, the ILP, the BSP, the Socialist
Labour Party (SLP), the National Union of Railwaymen and, of
course, the WSF. It also included Russian members who, for security reasons, were not to be named. The committee met above the
Dreadnought offices, at that time in Fleet Street. Its purpose, as its
name suggests, was to publish reliable information about Soviet
Russia, much of which came directly from that country and was
translated into English. In connection with this work Sylvia
earned the distinction of being the first person in Britain to
receive and publish an English translation of the Constitution of
the Soviet Republic.[3] Funding for the PRIB to the tune of £10 a
week came from Russian sources at the suggestion of Maxim
Litvinoff, the official Soviet representative in London. This
money was was to be obtained from Litvinoff's successor in
London, Theodore Rothstein.[4] Sylvia was not too fond of
Rothstein. Initially he greeted her 'ecstatically with an air of rev-
erential respect, almost adoration', but this was short lived as he
found her 'less powerful or maybe less pliable than he had anticipated'.[5] Sylvia recounted that the £10 subsidy 'did not go far. It
had to be supplemented by the efforts of the Committee and officials'[6] since at its height the organisation employed four workers
as well as having to meet costs of producing weekly circulars and
numerous pamphlets.

Communist Unity and the Communist Party of Great Britain

A turning point had been reached by revolutionary industrial
militants by 1919. The peculiar British paradox, that of a mass
movement without a political voice, and a tiny socialist (as

opposed to labourist) movement without mass support, was by now glaringly obvious. Syndicalism had shown itself capable of confronting individual employers, but not able to sustain lasting advance in the face of the full repressive power of the state. The war-time industrial struggles had witnessed the emergence of a much closer unity between some of the hitherto aloof socialist organisations like the SLP and the BSP with the shop stewards, but the special conditions of war, during which the state was forced to make concessions for its own survival, blurred the distinction between industrial and political action. The theories of Marx and Lenin, as well as the practical lessons of the Russian and German revolutions, pointed to the necessity of a united revolutionary socialist party to lead the movement to a more permanent advance in the battle against the capitalist system as a whole. The BSP can be credited with the many initiatives to forge unity between the various socialist organisations and the industrial militants. However, despite its later sectarianism, the WSF also deserves recognition as a force which, through its mass campaigning especially in defence of the Russian revolution, attempted to give practical expression to socialist unity. Whilst such recognition is long overdue, it would be erroneous to view the tortuous process of unity negotiations solely through the lens of the WSF. The WSF was only one of the socialist organisations involved in the formation of the Communist Party, and was, with a membership of 400–500 (mainly in the East End), the smallest. The ILP, involved in the talks in the early, but not the later, stages, was by far the largest with over 37,000 members. All the Marxist organisations were much smaller by comparison. The BSP, with around 6,000 members, led the field. The SLP, based mainly in Scotland, had roughly 1,200 members. The South Wales Socialist Society (SWSS, a descendant of the syndicalist Miners' Reform Movement) was a loose federal body without formal membership. However, the WSF's influence cannot be measured in membership terms alone. It derived in large part from the success of its weekly paper. As we have already seen the *Workers' Dreadnought* was refreshingly unsectarian and carried articles from all elements of the left regardless of affiliation. During and after the war it distinguished itself by its verve, openness and internationalism.[7] In 1918 the BSP had suggested that its paper, *The Call* should be amalgamated with the *Dreadnought*.[8] Although this was rejected 'at the present time', it is an indication of regard in which the paper was held.[9] The BSP and the

WSF continued to work closely together none the less. Indeed, according to Sylvia the BSP approached the WSF with 'a tentative offer of fusion, which was very cordially received'.[10] These talks did not get off the ground because of the fundamental disagreement between the two organisations on the question of participation in parliament.

The BSP had attempted a unity initiative in 1916 with the ILP and the Fabian Society. Unsurprisingly, the latter organisation refused to attend. The Russian revolution was a spur to renewed attempts and resulted in the formation of a United Socialist Council consisting of the BSP and the ILP. However, by 1919 it was clear that this had failed, largely because the BSP acknowledged what it regarded as an unhealable ideological rift between the two organisations. The October revolution had shown that it was vital to break with reformism and as a result the BSP position was that any advance towards the creation of a united socialist party was only possible on the basis of Marxism. This did not prevent unity in action on other issues, especially when it became clear that British troops were being used with those of other capitalist countries against the Bolshevik revolution. A powerful solidarity movement emerged in the form of the 'Hands Off Russia' Committee. Initiated by the BSP, SLP and left-wing shop stewards, it even won the support of the labour leadership. The Committee's president, A. A. Purcell, a member of the TUC's Parliamentary Committee, was also a member of the BSP. The WSF sent three delegates to the 'Hands Off Russia' conference held in January 1919. Practical solidarity, following intensive agitation, was shown by East London dockworkers when they refused in 1920 to load the 'Jolly George', a munitions ship destined for Russia. This could not have been accomplished without patient preparatory work. The agitation on the London docks had been organised by the WSF which ensured a steady stream of pro-Soviet literature reached the hands of the dockers. Harry Pollitt, later to become General Secretary of the Communist Party of Great Britain (CPGB), was a member of the WSF in 1919 when he moved to Poplar and was involved in this campaign : 'day after day we were posting up placards, stickybacks and posters on the dock-sides ... Sylvia Pankhurst kept us continuously supplied with copies of Lenin's *Appeal to the Toiling Masses.*'[11] 'Hands Off Russia' literature was sold. Pollitt had great admiration for Sylvia and the WSF, whose members he described as 'some of the most self-sacrificing and hard-working it has been my fortune to come into contact with'.[12] The threat that Britain might actually declare war against the Soviet Republic resulted, in August 1920, in the formation of Councils of Action (over 350 were established in all parts of the country, largely based on trades councils), which pledged, with the support of the TUC and the Labour Party, to mobilise mass strikes should the threat of war prove real.

In this atmosphere, the talk of communist unity became at once more urgent and more realistic. The establishment of the Third (Communist) International in Moscow in 1919 gave added impetus to the project. Known as the Comintern, the Third International (1919–43) was an expression of the ideological rift between communists and social democrats. In this sense it was not simply a replacement for the Second International (1889–1914) which had collapsed with the outbreak of the First World War, but a reflection of the already existing differences between rival schools of socialist thought. Such ideological differences had, by 1919–20, resulted in splits within most European workers' parties and the formation of separate communist and social democratic parties. The effect of the war, which had accentuated divisions between the 'incorporated' leaderships of the European labour movement and rank-and-file workers, together with the influence of the Russian revolution, were the deciding factors promoting a new kind of international organisation which explicitly rejected reformism and was based instead on a revolutionary Marxist world outlook. Adherence to the Comintern and its 21 principles, which were drafted by Lenin and adopted at the second Comintern Congress in 1920, provided a basis for ideological unity by explictly ruling out affiliation from centrist or reformist parties. The fundamentals were there – all participating organisations were self-selecting on this basis. Did they accept the dictatorship of the proletariat? Did they reject class collaboration? Did they support the principle of soviets in general and Soviet Russia in particular? If they agreed with all this they were communists and could participate in the talks.

These developments influenced the progress and the form of the communist unity discussions which had already begun in Britain. In June 1919 the unity process recommenced with a meeting of representatives of the four Marxist organisations, the BSP, the SLP, the WSF and the SWSS. However, agreement in theory (and *on* theory) proved to be much easier than agreement on strategy. These talks and those in the following year were bedevilled by disagreement over two major issues –

whether or not to affiliate to the Labour Party and whether or not to participate in local and parliamentary elections. Given that the WSF played a major role in these debates it is appropriate to examine its position more closely.

The WSF

As we have already seen, the WSF had been moving steadily, since 1917, in an anti-parliamentary direction. This was not a particularly unusual position on the British left. Opposition to 'bourgeois' parliament had been one of the motivating forces behind the pre-war syndicalist movement and continued into some sections of the still-active shop stewards' and workers' committee movement. Far from being a position adopted by the middle-class intelligentsia, it could be argued that it was a stance which was more in tune with class-conscious workers than the older, more 'incorporated' tradition. Willie Gallacher, the leader of the Clyde Workers' Committee (and later a Communist MP) strongly opposed parliamentary activity at this stage and argued his case at the Second Congress of the Communist International held in Moscow in 1920.[13] This fact did not necessarily bestow any greater credibility to the anti-parliamentary line, but it certainly lent it weight, coming as it did from the leader of the strongest rank-and-file workers' organisation in Britain at the time. Indeed, there may have been a certain amount of 'workerism' in Sylvia's conversion to the anti-parliamentary cause. The point is, however, that hers was not the isolated position which it is often claimed to be, although it could be argued, with some justification, that she pursued her line in a sectarian fashion. Similarly on the question of affiliation to the Labour Party. There is no doubt that Labour's record during the war, when it supported the draconian anti-strike measures of the government, alienated it from the socialist tide sweeping the labour movement. In this sense Sylvia was a late convert to the anti-Labour cause. She was, together with Melvina Walker, a WSF delegate to the Labour Party Women's Conference in May 1918, although that is not to say that she had any illusions about the political differences. In respect of the affiliation, the question had to be answered as to whether the Labour Party, as a federal organisation with trade union affiliates, could claim to represent, in one form, the mass of British workers. As it turned out this latter issue, although divisive, was highly theoretical, because when, after its formation in 1921, the Communist Party applied for affiliation to the Labour Party, it was turned down. None the less, the BSP was already affiliated to the Labour Party and had conducted a referendum of its members on this matter. Harry Pollitt, a member of the BSP, was hostile to retaining affiliation. He even travelled back to his native Openshaw to sway the BSP branch there (successfully) against affiliation.[14]

What has to be disentangled, therefore, in making an estimation of Sylvia's contribution at this time, is not so much her position on these two issues – many others had similar misgivings – but her strategy and tactics in pursuing them. Even then it seems clear that Sylvia came in for more than her fair share of opprobrium – a fact which may not be unconnected with her gender. Whilst a concern with Sylvia's psyche is not the concern of this book, one cannot but agree with her own frequently expressed view of herself that 'her decision making was uninfluenced by others'.[15] The positive aspect of this trait surfaced when she was running her own organisation on her own terms, but its negative side was apparent when her independence was threatened. This is not enough, however, to explain the obduracy which resulted ultimately in her setting up a rival communist party, disbanding it, joining the CPGB and then being expelled from it within six months.

Sylvia Pankhurst and Lenin

The WSF decided to apply for affiliation to the Third International immediately and was sharply critical of the ILP position, taken at its annual conference in Huddersfield in 1919, which declared in favour of a revival of the Second International and hence ruled itself out of discussions on communist unity. This was a matter of some regret for Sylvia, given her early close associations with the founder of that party. She wrote, 'The ILP has stepped out of the Socialist ranks and joined the Liberal reformists. It is a pity for much effort and sacrifice by many genuine socialists went into the building up of that Party, and this resolution is in direct conflict with the spirit of its founder Keir Hardie.'[16]

As secretary of the first British organisation to affiliate to the Comintern, Sylvia wrote to Lenin in July 1919 with an account of the various socialist groups and currents extant in Britain at the time. Of the seven groups she listed and assessed (primarily respecting their attitude to parliament) she regarded 'the revolutionary industrial workers' as 'the most hopeful elements'. She made no special claims for her own WSF. In addition, she asked his advice on the vexed question of participation in parliament and expressed strongly her own opinion that the 'movement in Great Britain is ruined by Parliamentarism' and was holding back the creation of a communist party . She was roundly attacked by the BSP[17] for having the temerity to take this independent initiative, especially since her letter was published in *Communist International*,[18] the official journal of the Comintern Executive. It appeared anonymously, with an editorial note explaining that the letter was written by 'an English comrade, a well-known Communist' and that it and Lenin's reply were sent to the journal by Lenin himself on account of the 'extreme importance' of the two documents.[19] Given that Sylvia's letter ruffled so many BSP feathers at the time and that the two letters have acquired such historical importance, it is worthwhile considering them more closely. The BSP claimed in *The Call*[20] that it was publishing the full text of both letters. This was not in fact the case. The original version, which appeared in the English edition of the *Communist International*, bore only a loose resemblance to the 'retranslated' rendering. Much of the sense was the same, save in a few important particulars. For example, in the original letter, the first political group identified by Sylvia was the Labour Party and not, as *The Call* said, 'Trade Unionists and Labour politicians'. Furthermore she did *not* say that the BSP was 'even more hopeless than the Independents' (i.e. the ILP), rather that it 'is often little better from the Communist outlook'. There are numerous other inaccuracies, the most important being the characterisation of the role of the WSF. In the original letter Sylvia reported accurately that although at its annual conference at Whitsun 1919 the WSF had transformed itself into a Communist Party, 'it was agreed that it should continue to work under the old name for the present, pending the results of the efforts that are being made to form a united Communist Party'. This is very different from the BSP version which sought to place the WSF in a highly sectarian light. Its 'retranslation' read that the WSF, instead of changing its name, decided

> to make all efforts to organise a united Communist Party by amalgamating the third [BSP], fifth [SLP], sixth [WSF], and

seventh group with the co-operation of the fourth group ['revolutionary industrialists'], the fourth group being the South Wales Socialist Society. Some are of the opinion that it will prove impossible to induce the SLP to join a Communist Party, though certain of its members may do so.

This section was thus a pure invention designed to create the impression that Sylvia at this stage was going it alone. It was, of course, *The Call*'s version of the letter which gained currency. The BSP was scathing in its attack on Sylvia at this time, claiming that she was doing little to bring about unity and had an inflated idea about her own importance. Fred Willis, editor of *The Call*, claimed that the BSP, more than any other political party, was distinctively working class (having 'shed its "bourgeois intellectuals" during the war') and hence 'possesses the qualities and the limitations of the working class'.[21] A mere 'bourgeois like Miss Pankhurst cannot understand this. She imagines that she is "the party of the poor" because she carries on a street corner propaganda and has her headquarters in the East End.' He went on to say that this didn't make her party any more revolutionary than the Salvation Army which also had its headquarters in the East End and organised street corner activity. Furthermore, Sylvia was criticised for not having printed Lenin's reply to her letter, a strange charge since her original was not intended for publication. *The Call* printed Lenin's reply. In it he demonstrated his understanding that anti-parliamentarism was a widely held position on the British left, particularly among advanced workers and that, although he thought that British workers should participate in elections, this was secondary to the main issue of forming a united communist party. Indeed Lenin argued that it would be a mistake for those in the BSP who are 'convinced Bolsheviks' and who hold a pro-parliamentary line, to hold up the formation of the Communist Party on this issue alone: 'the mistake such Bolsheviks will make will ... be a thousandfold greater than of those who refuse to participate in the elections for a British bourgeois Parliament'. This was certainly weaker than the line Lenin took less than a year later in *Left Wing Communism* in which he argued that British Communists should unite on the basis of the principles of the Third International 'and of *obligatory* participation in parliament'.[22]

Unity Talks

The question of whether or not to participate in local and parliamentary elections was a particularly sensitive issue in the unity talks which had recommenced in May 1919. Despite Sylvia's misgivings, there is little doubt that the WSF's decision to participate in these and those held in 1920 was influenced by Lenin's response to Sylvia's letter. An appendix to the Official Report of the Communist Unity Convention of 1920,[23] written by Albert Inkpin, gave the background of the 14 months of negotiations. The Provisional Committee, set up in June 1919 and consisting of the four Marxist organisations (including the WSF), aware of the major tactical differences on elections and Labour Party affiliation, decided to adopt a 'middle course'. The affiliation question was to be 'settled by the new Party when it is formed'.[24] Although this was acceptable to the WSF,[25] Inkpin notes that its (i.e. the WSF's) anti-parliamentarism 'suddenly became a fetish' and as a consequence its attitude became 'more and more lukewarm and later, distinctly hostile'.[26]

The pages of the *Workers' Dreadnought* resounded with a withering attack on the Labour Party. Sylvia asked, rhetorically, why, given that the Third International had rejected the Labour Party as affiliates, British communists should seek union with an organisation rejected by the Comintern. In a long article[27] explaining the WSF position, Sylvia took issue with Inkpin's (BSP) characterisation of the Labour Party as 'the main body of the working-class movement'. Instead she described the Party as typifying 'social patriotic working-class parties of bourgeois outlook'. She contrasted its programme with the revolutionary programme and, naturally, found it wanting. The Labour Party would, she argued, 'inevitably come to power' and thus it would be futile 'to dissipate our energy' in 'adding to its strength'. She noted that throughout Europe splits were taking place between communists and social democrats and wondered why, therefore, the BSP line was so contrary to the general revolutionary trend. Perhaps the BSP thought it would be possible to win over the Labour Party for a revolutionary position. If so, in Sylvia's opinion this was a disastrously mistaken hope since the Labour Party was not open to democratic influence. In fact 'in all of Europe there is no social patriotic organisation so carefully guarded for social patriotism as the British Labour Party'. Furthermore the Labour Party was the least socialist of all the social democratic parties – it was the last to join the Second International and was hostile to the Russian revolution.

Certainly Sylvia's argument had a logic to it and in purely descriptive terms was not far wide of the mark. However, the key point which Sylvia missed in this account was any appreciation of the truly unique feature of the British Labour Party: namely that it was connected for better or for worse to the labour movement via its organic link with the trade unions. The unions had been instrumental in both the formation and the maintenance of the party. In this sense Inkpin was correct in describing the Party as 'the main body of the movement'. There was no parallel to this in Europe (with the possible exception of Belgium) and thus drawing lessons on this question from elsewhere was inappropriate. Pre-figuring her action to be taken four months later, Sylvia ended her anti-Labour Party article with the call to build a communist party: 'in the meantime', she went on, 'we must persevere with communist propaganda and never hesitate lest we make it too extreme ... the more extreme our doctrine is, the more surely we will prepare the workers for communism.'

Clearly, Labour Party affiliation was a thorny and divisive matter. Again a compromise was suggested during the unity negotiations which would have placed this issue before a special rank-and-file convention, but the BSP insisted that a declaration in favour of a united communist party would have to be achieved first, otherwise the whole process of unity would have reverted to its original divided starting point. The WSF objected to this and withdrew from the Provisional Committee. This action of the WSF was rendered more unaccountable by Sylvia's decision in June 1920 to go it alone and establish her own communist party. Obviously Inkpin viewed this with hostility: 'such disruptive action deserves the severest condemnation.'[28] Although, given these circumstances, one would not expect his assessment of the new Communist Party, British Section of the Third International (CP(BSTI)), as the WSF now called itself, to be favourable, there is little reason to doubt that its founding conference was 'a tiny and uninfluential gathering'.[29] One of the 'delegates' to the conference described the event as 'fatuous fooling'.[30] Dave Ramsey of the workers' committee movement, a leading London shop steward and anti-parliamentarian, similarly condemned 'the disruptionist movement that has led to the re-formation of the WSF under the title (impudently assumed) of the Communist Party BSTI'.[31]

What induced Sylvia to take this sectarian course at such a critical juncture in the unity process is matter of some speculation.
It cannot be accounted for purely in relation to the disagreements on the issues alone, since others who shared Sylvia's views
did not drop out at this point, and indeed great efforts were made
to accommodate the differences, if only by postponing final decisions on them for the sake of preserving unity. Pelling[32]
considers that she was fearful of being outvoted by the stronger
BSP, while Winslow[33] accounts for her action by tracing her link,
through the influence and contacts of her Italian anarchist
partner Silvio Corio, with ultra-left, anti-parliamentary European
socialists. She made the acquaintance of such 'leftists'[34] when
she travelled (clandestinely) to various European countries in
1919. These were heady days – the German and Hungarian revolutions had not yet been defeated and with factory occupations
in Italy there seemed a real possibility of working-class power. In
Amsterdam in July she attended an international conference of
the 'ultra left' which opposed parliamentarism and called for an
international 24-hour general strike to oppose armed intervention by the capitalist countries against the Russian and
Hungarian revolutions.[35] It is interesting to note that Fred Willis
of the BSP (editor of *The Call*) was a delegate to this conference –
an indication of the fluidity of left politics during this new period
of communist formation ushered in by the Russian revolution.
However, despite such influences and the countervailing ones
provided by the leading German socialist feminist Clara Zetkin
(whom she met in Frankfurt during this time) and Lenin, both of
whom she admired enormously, Sylvia's position was ultimately
out of step with almost everyone. The fact is that she elevated tactical and strategic differences into differences of *principle* and this
not only led to her isolation from the unity process, but ultimately from communist and socialist politics altogether. This
can only be explained by acknowledging that despite her enormous achievements as an agitator and organiser, her grasp of
Marxist theory (what Lenin regarded as the basis for revolutionary action) was weak and that whilst she undoubtedly had both
sympathy and contact with workers, her politics in this regard
were voluntarist and displayed both an impatience and a lack of
understanding of the historic forms of workers' organisations.
Building a women's movement, where none had existed, was a
different matter from finding ways to influence a long-established (and sometimes incorporated) labour movement with all
its imperfections. Although her impatience with this tradition

was understandable, particularly in the heady revolutionary atmosphere of the post-1917 period, two caveats must be made. First, her impatience was unwarranted given that a significant break from the plodding reformist tradition was at last being made as witnessed by the spectacular growth and influence of the shop stewards' and workers' committee movement – a development generated *within* the official movement, the repercussions of which, in terms of the future orientation of the labour movement, had yet to be tested. Second, Sylvia had displayed much more patience, from her perspective, with the infinitely more flawed position of the WSPU in which she had continued to work over a long period without giving public voice to her differences until she was expelled in 1914.

Thus Sylvia excluded herself from the Communist Unity Convention held in the summer of 1920. In any case she was not in England at the time – she was in Moscow as a delegate from her organisation to the Second Congress of the Third International. It was a dangerous journey for her since she had no visa and thus travelled illegally and uncomfortably. At the very time that Sylvia, Gallacher and others were arguing the toss with Lenin about affiliation and parliament, the CPGB was holding its founding congress. A wireless message was received in London from Lenin to the Congress. It stated baldly:

> I consider the policy of Comrade Sylvia Pankhurst and of the Workers' Socialist Federation in refusing to collaborate in the amalgamation of the British Socialist Party, Socialist Labour Party and others into a Communist Party to be wrong.

It continued:

> I am personally in favour of participation in Parliament and of adhesion to the Labour Party on condition of free and independent communist activity ... I consider it most desirable that a Communist Party be speedily organised on the basis of the decisions and principles of the Third International and that the Party be brought into close touch with the Industrial Workers of the World and Shop Stewards' Committees in order to bring about their complete union.[36]

Lenin's intervention was decisive, although in spite of it, the issue of Labour Party affiliation was carried at the CPGB congress only by a small majority. The decision to participate in parliamentary elections was, however, passed overwhelmingly. Undoubtedly, Lenin's position during the debates in Moscow also had an impact on both Sylvia and Gallacher. It is clear that Sylvia felt the conference gave her a fair hearing, indeed she was permitted at one point 'to extend to twenty-five minutes, the allotted five minutes'[37] for speeches. Lenin took her arguments seriously, 'as though our defeat had not been a foregone conclusion'.[38] It is quite evident, reading Lenin's speech[39] at the Congress, that he appreciated the uniqueness of the British situation. He had no doubt that the British Labour Party was led by 'bourgeois elements, of social traitors', but at the same time the fact that it allowed the BSP to remain in its ranks meant that there was freedom to state this openly and thus to influence the many thousands of workers who were affiliated to it through their trade unions. In answer to Gallacher's criticism that the BSP was 'hopelessly reformist', Lenin argued that if this was true (which he doubted), the way to change it was by inducing the revolutionary workers of Glasgow 'to straighten out its tactics in the spirit of the resolutions that have been adopted here'. In response to Sylvia's fear that real revolutionaries would be expelled from the Labour Party, Lenin's response was 'that this would not be a bad thing at all', indeed 'it would be a great victory for the communist and labour movement in England [sic]' because it would show that they were powerful enough to be feared.

The effect of this debate, which effectively set what had become a sterile strategic argument in a revolutionary context, induced Sylvia upon her return to Britain to disband her own organisation and join, albeit briefly, the CPGB. Willie Gallacher had been won round and Sylvia may also have been influenced by his letter to her[40] in which he argued as a parliamentary 'abstentionist' that it would be possible to continue the discussion about parliament within the party, and that if they were successful in winning it round to the anti-parliamentary line they would then have the opportunity to influence the world communist movement. If the CP (BSTI) stayed out, argued Gallacher, it would be marginalised: 'inside you can do much. Outside your efforts will be mostly wasted.' He countered what he anticipated might be Sylvia's position that the CP (BSTI) should stay out until the world movement came round to its point of view by suggesting that members 'should ask themselves if it will not come round very much quicker if they are inside'. He urged her to assist him on this great task of 'shaping the policy of the international movement', which he thought would be possible by the next world congress given that by that time 'the experiences of our comrades in many countries may bring them round to the support of the abstentionist thesis'. Such was the perspective offered by Gallacher and was a clear indication of the value he placed (at this stage anyway) on Sylvia's work.

However, the fact was that Sylvia's tiny Communist Party was never effective and had virtually ceased to function anyway, although the *Workers' Dreadnought* was still going strong. None the less, at its National Inaugural Conference in Manchester in September 1920, the CP (BSTI) was persuaded by Sylvia to follow the Comintern's advice and participate in further unity talks. The CPGB also discussed the Comintern Congress and acted on its call for a further unity convention to include all those groups which had hitherto remained outside. Although Sylvia accepted this initative, her ability to operate effectively (if at all) was rendered impossible because she was arrested in October 1920 on charges of sedition arising from articles in the *Dreadnought* which, it was alleged, incited mutiny among the armed forces. She was imprisoned from October 1920 until May 1921. During the period of her imprisonment her organisation[41] along with the Communist Labour Party (a new group formed by Gallacher from various elements of Scottish shop stewards' and revolutionary groups) and the national shop stewards' and workers' committee movement joined with the CPGB in organising and calling a Unity Convention to be held in Leeds in January 1921.

The Workers' Dreadnought: Sylvia's Expulsion

The CPGB paper, *The Communist* (previously *The Call*) published a full report of the Leeds Unity Conference under the banner headline 'The Communist Parties are dead: *Long Live the Communist Party*'.[42] However, forming a united party was one thing – establishing it in practice was another. Sylvia had hoped that she would still be able to fight for her 'left' line within the new organisation, as Gallacher had suggested. She advocated the formation of a 'left bloc' which 'should have its own convenors, and its own special sittings prior to the Party Conference, to decide its policy'.[43] Despite her claim that Lenin had told her that he approved of such a policy,[44] Sylvia had little support for such a perspective, including from Edgar Whitehead, former secretary of the CP (BSTI) and now a member of the CPGB executive.[45] She was, apparently, quite undaunted by such isolation – indeed it seemed to confirm her line, especially since she now asserted that there were non-communist elements both within the CPGB and in the CP (BSTI), thus serving to confirm the need for a left bloc. Although the CP (BSTI) no longer existed after the Leeds conference, the *Workers' Dreadnought* did, thus raising the question of whether it was an officially approved CPGB publication. The CP (BSTI) had already, for reasons of it own, attempted to control the *Dreadnought*. Having failed in this, the CP (BSTI) had ultimately 'decided to repudiate it [i.e. the *Dreadnought*] as official organ of the Communist Party BSTI, and also to institute a boycott' against it and its printer, the Agenda Press.[46] For her part, Sylvia argued that the paper had never been the official organ of the CP (BSTI): it was her paper and she had merely allowed the party to use it. Hence once the CP (BSTI) had decided to merge as part of the CPGB, Sylvia argued 'the conditions under which I placed the *Workers' Dreadnought* at the disposal of the Party as its organ, will have ceased to operate.'[47] This theme was developed in subsequent articles in which it was argued that the paper, now edited by Nora Smyth during Sylvia's imprisonment, had always been an independent organ and had only been 'lent' to the CP (BSTI) which 'never made itself responsible for any part of the burden of maintaining it'.[48] This reasoning did not cut much ice with the CPGB, which was faced with the daunting prospect of each individual party and group bringing its own periodical with it into the new unified organisation. Clearly this was impractical and undesirable if the Party was to speak with one voice, although it should be noted three such papers were permitted to continue, notably *Plebs*, *Solidarity* and the *Worker*. The *Workers' Dreadnought*, with its still substantial circulation, could hardly be considered in the same category as the broadsheets of the tiny left groups. In any case, it was no longer the official organ of any group. Sylvia did not share the CPGB's concerns about the control of papers and periodicals. She had a pluralist attitude to the communist press and argued that it was both impossible and undesirable for the official party organ to do everything – to appeal to the masses and to serve the needs of the party at the same time. It is interesting to note in this connection that she regarded the *Dreadnought*'s appeal as being 'more largely to Communists who already understand the fundamentals of communism and the class war and need more advanced matter'.[49] Hence, the *Dreadnought* seemed to be arguing that, in effect, it was or should be regarded as the chief theoretical organ of the party – a surprising line given that the paper had always distinguished itself by its mass appeal, especially to women. Clearly such a position was hardly likely to find favour with the new leadership of the CPGB.

Sylvia made matters worse, in the eyes of the CPGB leadership, by permitting the paper's continued advocacy of factional activity within the CPGB and its characterisation of the new Party as a BSP takeoveover in which Hyndmanism[50] was still rampant. In addition, the paper began to be critical of the Comintern. It published material from 'ultra lefts' outside Britain, including a long series of articles by the Dutch communist Herman Gorter entitled: 'An open letter to Comrade Lenin: an answer to Lenin's brochure "Left Wing Communism an Infantile Disorder"'.

As it was, the CPGB deferred a decision on whether or not to 'approve' the *Dreadnought* until Sylvia was released from prison. She was then called to meet a sub-committee of the Executive Committee. She reported this meeting in a long article in the *Dreadnought* headlined 'Freedom of discussion'.[51] In it she described the two options presented to her by the CPGB in respect of her paper – either to cease publication altogether or to hand it over to the Party under the editorship of someone of the Party's choosing. She rejected both options. She wrote of the meeting with the leadership that, 'with a spice of brutality, the disciplinarians set forth their terms to one who had for eight years maintained a pioneer paper with constant struggle and in the face of much persecution'. She justified her rejection of the Party's proposal on the grounds that 'an independent Communist paper which would stimulate discussion in the movement on theory and practice' was an essential prerequisite of healthy Party life. She acknowledged that Party discipline could and should be used to 'prevent right opportunism and laxity', but suppressing discussion of left-wing ideas would 'cramp and stultify' the Party. It was only permissible, she argued, to prevent such discussion in a revolutionary situation, but she 'could not approve of a rigidity of discipline which is wholly out of place here and now'.

However the real clue to the disagreement lay perhaps not in such abstractions, but on the concrete 'left-wing' issues which she espoused and to which the *Dreadnought* would continue to

give expression. Prime among these were the hoary old chest-
nuts of opposition to parliament and to Labour Party affiliation.
In addition she identified something new; namely the duty of
her paper to give a platform to the Workers' Opposition in
Soviet Russia. She claimed that Russia was drifting to the right
and had 'permitted the re-introduction of many features of capitalism' giving rise to strong differences of view among Russian
communists and within the Third International. Thus Sylvia
was not simply arguing that her paper had the right to continue
as an independent communist journal, but one which was
actively pursuing a line at variance with the CPGB and the
mainstream of the international movement. Given that the
fledgling British Party operated on the basis of democratic cen-
tralism, Sylvia was in fact arguing that she had the right to
pursue factional activity and as such was bound on a collision
course, notwithstanding opinions on the merits of her case.
Thus it was that Sylvia was expelled from the CPGB. A brief
report in *The Communist*[52] was the first and last mention of the
expulsion. It stated that the disciplinary action taken against
her on 10 September, was on the following grounds:

> The Executive requested Miss Pankhurst to hand the paper
> over to the control of the Party ... Miss Pankhurst gave a def-
> inite and explicit refusal to do so. The Executive expressed
> regret at her action, but was of the opinion that such a
> breach of discipline could not be tolerated and expelled Miss
> Pankhurst accordingly. Branches are requested to observe
> this action, and to note that the *Workers' Dreadnought* is not
> a Party organ.

The *Dreadnought* printed several letters in September and
October of 1921 regretting her expulsion, including one from
her staunch ally Nora Smyth, who announced that since she
held the same views as Sylvia she presumed that she too was
expelled from the CPGB. Willie Gallacher also wrote[53] repeating
the claim, vehemently denied by Sylvia, that she had counted
on her expulsion as a means of increasing her popularity in
anti-CPGB circles, thereby gaining 'financial assistance' for her
paper.[54]

Sylvia counted her breach with the CPGB as the 'seventh
decision' which had influenced her life.[55] Having (with characteristic lack of modesty) stated she had done 'more than any
other single individual here to pioneer the way' which made a

communist party possible, to then join it 'would have been to reap something of the hard effort I had made in sowing. To refuse that course meant much isolation and brought upon me vulgar attacks.' So why did she do it? As has been mentioned earlier, she was by no means the only one who had tactical and strategic differences with the CPGB and the Comintern, but she was the first (in Britain) to be expelled for them. Her own individualism was a factor to which she herself gave credence: 'always I obeyed my sense of right. I consulted no-one, thought out my position, stated it, acted upon it.'[56] After her expulsion she attempted to explain her political difference with the CPGB in an article entitled 'Our point of view'.[57] This was a confused piece in which she repeated the old arguments about parliament and the Labour Party and added a new element of criticism relating to the establishment in 1921 of the Red International of Labour Unions (RILU).[58] This organisation, consisting of affiliates of class-conscious, pro-Soviet official and unofficial trade union organisations and groups, was set up in opposition to the reformist International Federation of Trade Unions (1919). Sylvia criticised it because it was not a solely rank-and-file organisation and considered that it was tainted by the inclusion of representatives of the official movement. In so doing she missed the point entirely. It was precisely because of the strength of the unofficial movement, which had developed during the war, that many unions had been pushed into adopting a non-collaborationsist position and, understanding this dynamic, the *raison d'être* of the RILU was to forge a unity between the rank and file and any emerging progressive leadership in order to detach the latter from organised reformism in the form of the alternative international, the International Federation of Trade Unions. The same article contained a contradictory and confused attitude to the Communist International. On the one hand, Sylvia criticised communists for not operating the policy of the Third International, especially in relation to the immediacy of the revolutionary transformation and the break with reformism, but on the other hand she contended that 'the present policy of the Third International is illogical and unworkable, and either the policy must be changed, or a new force must arise to achieve the workers' revolution outside Russia, and to make Russia herself a Communist country'.

Infected by the pessimism of 'Black Friday' Sylvia's faith in the revoluionary rank and file also appeared to be waning.

'Black Friday' was the name given by militants to the failure of the planned general strike in April 1921 of the 'Triple Alliance' of mine, railway and transport workers in support of the miners' protest against savage wage cuts. It was called off at the last minute due to the back-stage manoeuvring of the trade union leaders, notably J. H. Thomas of the railwaymen (later a Labour MP). Shortly after her expulsion, Sylvia announced the 'Death of the old industrialism'.[59] As well as attacking A. J. Cook, the militant miners' leader, Sylvia appeared to write off industrial action in almost the same tones as she criticised participation in elections. She declared that industrial unionism, by which she meant 100 per cent union membership, was a spent force and with it the strike weapon:

> Cook and his school refuse to realise that since the strike weapon the only effective weapon ever wielded by the old industrial unionism is powerless now, the old industrial unionism is itself deprived of power. Cook and his school cannot adapt themselves to the changed position; they cannot discover new tactics.[60]

The 'new tactics' she advocated, however, were hardly new. It consisted of a call to by-pass trade unions altogether and 'make revolution'.

Perhaps more surprisingly, Sylvia was lukewarm about the struggle on her own doorstep in Poplar. The majority of the councillors in the London Borough of Poplar refused to levy the local rate until there was some measure of rate equalisation between the very rich and the poor boroughs. This protest, known as Poplarism, resulted in the imprisonment in 1921 of 30 councillors, among whom were close associates of Sylvia in the women's suffrage and anti-war struggles in the East End. These included Nellie Cressall, Julia Scurr, George and Minnie Lansbury and Jennie Mackay. It may be that her lack of enthusiasm was explained by her long-standing ambivalence to George Lansbury, now the mayor of Poplar. Sylvia's hostility to the National Unemployed Workers' (Committee) Movement (NUW(C)M) from its inception in 1921 is, however, easier to explain. She regarded it as a communist front organisation, and, given the resentment she felt about her expulsion from the CPGB, she was, for a short while, very anti-communist. She misjudged the nature of the NUW(C)M, which was a broad-based activist organisation of the type that the ELFS used to be.

Indeed, one of the paid organisers of the NUW(C)M, Lillian Thring, had worked closely with Sylvia in the ELFS. In 1923, Sylvia made the sectarian mistake of establishing a rival organisation, the Unemployed Workers' Organisation (UWO), whose slogan, 'Abolition of the Wages System', was supposed to expose the 'reformist' nature of the demand of its rival – 'Work or Full Maintenance'. The UWO collapsed within a year.

Women and Communism

Thus far it would appear that Sylvia's feminism was entirely engulfed by the all consuming tide of revolutionary politics on the national and international stage in the post-war period. Whilst there were doubtless many women activists in this arena, there were very few women leaders, and even fewer who regarded themselves as socialist feminists. Clara Zetkin in Germany and Alexandra Kollontai in Russia, together with Sylvia, were among the few who combined their revolutionary socialism with a feminist perspective. For these women the system of soviets or workers' councils, ushered in by the Russian revolution and adopted in embryonic form by the rank-and-file workers' movements throughout Europe, offered great hopes for the liberation of women. Sylvia attempted to give expression, albeit in theoretical terms, to a socialist feminist perspective in her 'Constitution for British soviets. Points for a communist programme'.[62] In this she advanced the idea that soviets should be based not just on the workplace but in all spheres of human activity, including the household so that 'mothers and those who are the organisers of the family life of the community may be adequately represented'. Her plan was that every urban and rural area should be divided into household soviet areas of roughly 250 people, run by women. These household soviets would be responsible for such issues as cooperative housekeeping, children's nurseries, supplies of food and clothing and all manner of social provision. She also envisaged the formation of education, public health and military soviets. These, together with industrial soviets, would send delegates to the district soviets which would coordinate the work of all of them and play their role as 'the instrument of the proletarian dictatorship against capitalism'. This was undoubtedly a sincere attempt to ensure that women's voices were heard during and after the revolutionary process. It also reflects Sylvia's commitment to a non-parliamentary form of direct democracy which linked locality and workplace and was based on her many years of experience of local campaigning in the East End. At the same time, however, her vision also revealed a surprising degree of acceptance of the traditional sexual division of labour. Although she insisted that workers of both sexes and all grades should form the workers' (not workmen's) committees in each workshop, it is clear that at worst she regarded work outside the home as primarily a masculine undertaking and at best she paid insufficient attention to the particular issues of segregated female labour. This would have entailed more serious consideration of the contradictions faced by women workers in combining their roles in social production with their function in the family. It would also have necessitated a more thoroughgoing analysis of the specifics of female paid labour which was often not performed in conventional 'workshops', but rather in unregulated sweatshops or as homeworkers employed on a piecework basis. This is not to diminish Sylvia's contribution as one of the very few efforts to combine revolutionary socialism and feminism in Britain at the time, but equally the claim that feminism was central to her thinking[62] in this period cannot be substantiated. Rather, in characteristerically pragmatic form she attempted to fit what she perceived as the needs of women into her central vision of a version of revolutionary syndicalism mediated by the concept of social soviets. Women were thus to play a role, an important one in her scheme of things, in the social sphere. In this sense her version was not as gender blind as traditional syndicalism, but nevertheless it endorsed its acceptance of the sexual division of labour. Furthermore, although it cannot be doubted that women's equality was an important issue for Sylvia, it did not occupy the same position in her political work as it had done in previous years. Again this is not an historicist side-swipe, but an observation based on her as yet tentative understanding of the relationship between class exploitation and oppression. In the unfolding drama of the revolutionary process her preoccupation with the besetting questions of communist strategy pushed the concerns of women into the background. Most men (with the exception of Lenin and a few others) were content to leave them there. Sylvia was not, although the pages of her paper contained few articles of significance about women during this period. Sylvia's younger sister, Adela Pankhurst Walsh, an Executive Committee member of the Communist Party of Australia, wrote a major piece sub-titled 'Communists will abolish prostitution',[63] and Dora Montefiore (CPGB), in defiance of her own party's hostility to the *Dreadnought*, contributed an article explaining 'Why we celebrate a Communist Women's Day'.[64] In addition, the series written by Sylvia on 'Soviet Russia as I saw it' contained interesting material on cooperative housekeeping – a project favoured by Alexandra Kollontai, the Minister for Social Welfare in Soviet Russia in 1917 and later (1920) the leader of the Soviet Women's Organisation (the Zhenotdel). The *Dreadnought* reprinted many of Kollontai's articles, but most of them were in her capacity as one of the leaders of the Workers' Opposition in Soviet Russia – a cause which was increasingly important to Sylvia.

By August 1920, the Communist Party of Great Britain existed. It was, and for many years remained, tiny. Its influence, however, was immeasurably greater than the sum total of its membership. From the very beginning it had within its ranks the leading industrial militants who had led the massive pre-war strikes and who had formed the core of the shop stewards' movement during the war. To these were added either in 1920 or later other individuals and small groups who had either been 'converted' to Marxism or induced to jettison pure syndicalism because of the war and the Russian revolution. The SWSS, and some of the Guild Socialists (like R. Page Arnot, Ellen Wilkinson and Walter Holmes) fell into this latter category. A left-wing group within the ILP, including such individuals as Shapurji Saklatvala, R. Palme Dutt, Emile Burns and Helen Crawfurd, may be counted among the former.

It would be wrong to lay any false claims about the significance of the formation of the Communist Party in 1920, given the stranglehold of the by-now well-entrenched reformist and labourist traditions in Britain. Such traditions, nurtured and abetted by social imperialism, had deprived Marxism of a mass following. Equally, however, it would be wrong to deny the importance of the Communist Party's existence. For at least 60 years it was the only significant Marxist organisation in Britain providing a focus for the activities of the left politically and industrially. As such it was a force with which the ruling class and the right-wing labour leadership had constantly to reckon. Whatever its defects it could hardly be characterised as an organisation 'dominated by opportunists'[65] as one of Sylvia's milder criticisms suggested. Her own revolutionary communist phase ended when the *Workers' Dreadnought* ceased publication in 1924. Thereafter her politics moved to the right, although she remained an unaligned socialist.

6

Anti-imperialism, Anti-racism and Anti-fascism

Sylvia Pankhurst is known primarily as a socialist feminist. However, one aspect of her work which has received scant attention is that of anti-racism. Although there is little in her writings to elucidate this, there is much in her practice which shows that she had an understanding of race oppression which was unusual, if not unique, for a white political activist of her time. In 1912, when she visited the USA on a speaking tour on women's suffrage, she addressed an audience at the Indian University in Arkansas and at the Negro University in Tennessee. It was unusual for a white woman to do this and she found that every newspaper protested against her action. It would seem that her empathy for the rights of black people arose from her commitment to women's rights which had led her to an understanding of the nature of oppression in general. This, combined with her socialism and internationalism, helped to free her from the chauvinism inherent in the socialisation of Britain's 'imperial race'.

Sylvia lived during the heyday of the British Empire, an Empire which had expanded enormously after the First World War when the defeated German Empire was divided between France and Britain. Although the black population in Britain was still small, racism was a predominant and virtually unquestioned feature of British thinking. Racist ideology was not confined to the ruling elite – it had profound resonances in all tiers of British society, including the labour movement and the women's movement.

Imperial Ideology, Eugenics and Racism

The ideology of racism had underpinned slavery and hence was not a new phenomenon. In the period of imperialist expansion, however, it was dressed up in a new pseudo-scientific garb and given a populist mass appeal. There was ample opportunity to disseminate the ideology given that the last quarter of the nineteenth century witnessed a great expansion, formally and informally, of the ideological apparatus of the state which was both prompted and facilitated by the rise in literacy (by 1890 elementary education was free and compulsory for all). This was the era of the birth, and the wide-scale development, of the popular press (dominated by the conservative magnate, Harmsworth), the propaganda poster, the music hall, the Scout movement (and other similar youth movements), the working mens' club, cheaper and more popular literature (the novels of Henty and Kipling) and great national pageants like Queen Victoria's diamond jubilee and Empire Day. School geography and history textbooks perpetrated racial supremacist dogma as established fact.[1]

The expanded mass culture, beginning in the last two decades of the nineteenth century, coincided with the vast expansion of the British Empire during the same period. Volumes of 'scholarly' writings appeared to provide some kind of intellectual justification of British racial superiority. Hitler was later to draw upon the writing of the British white supremacists of this era. Men like Benjamin Kidd and Karl Pearson subverted Darwin's theory of evolution by crudely using his ideas on the 'survival of the fittest' and applying them to the struggle between races. Despite the finer points of 'theory' which divided the two men, their central concern, born out of England's declining economic position as a world power, was the question of the national 'struggle for existence', which for them was synonymous with racial superiority. *Social Evolution*, published in 1894, had established Kidd's reputation as one of the leading British sociologists of the day. He regarded Marxism as the main enemy and believed that the granting of the vote to the working class and social legislation designed to improve the position of workers would damage the position of the wealthier classes and impel society in a socialist direction unless alternative mediating values replaced socialistic ones. For him, these values were religion and nationalism. Such values would inspire a devotion to the concept of duty which he counterposed to the individualism and self-seeking nature of the socialist ethic that, if left unchecked, would result in national stagnation. He asserted the superiority of the Anglo-Saxon race to which the English and the Germans belonged. This race, by virtue of its superior characteristics, had a higher 'social efficiency' which equipped it to triumph in the 'struggle for existence' on a world scale.

Karl Pearson, Professor of Applied Mathematics at University College, London, did not share Kidd's antipathy to Marxism. Pearson accepted much of Marx's economic teaching, but his objection to socialism was as the theory of class struggle and revolution. For this he substituted the struggle between races as the mechanism of progress. According to him the black races had already lost out in this struggle, having been conquered by the whites, hence proving the racial superiority of the conqueror. In order to prove this he created the new subject of biometrics – statistical biology. Pearson was popular among the left and was widely quoted in ILP literature and by ILP feminists like Isabella Ford.[2] Pearson associated himself with the biologist Francis Galton, a cousin of Charles Darwin and Professor of 'eugenics' at London University. Galton discovered this new 'science' of eugenics, the practical application of which could, by means of selective breeding, regulate heredity and produce a super (white) race, capable of surviving the struggle for existence. Eugenics became an established and virtually unquestioned orthodoxy. It was allied to the prevalent fear that the survival of the imperial super race was jeopardised by two problems: first the decline in the birth rate, which had fallen steadily, especially among the middle class, since the 1880s and second, the 'degenerated' condition of the masses. Galton, Kidd and Pearson therefore placed great emphasis on the role of race motherhood. This led Galton actively to oppose the women's suffrage movement, arguing that it diverted women from their primary task of childbearing and rearing. Other eugenicists took a different line. The feminist-eugenicist argument centred around the concern that race mothers, in order to fulfil their historic mission, needed to be educated and aware. Women's independence, provided it did not contradict motherhood, could be seen as a useful eugenic tool in that it would result in more suitable, well-matched marriages which would produce stronger stock.[3]

Concern for the Empire and the survival of the British race undoubtedly had an impact on the women's movement. Vron Ware argues convincingly that 'feminist ideology and practice were shaped by the social, economic and political forces of imperialism to a far greater extent than has been acknowledged'.[4] There are frequent references in suffrage literature to women's role as race mothers. Indeed, one of the arguments used by both the NUWSS and the WSPU to justify the demand for women's enfranchisement was that women needed the vote in order to ensure that parliament paid proper attention to the maintenance and survival of a healthy race. Who better to do this than women? Women's politics would concern itself with the agenda that men forgot – care of children, the sick and the elderly. The implicit presumption that these were 'women's issues' was not challenged by the mainstream women's movement. Christabel Pankhurst argued that women needed the vote because they had 'a service to render, to the state as well as the home, to the race as well as the family'.[5] Sylvia recognised this racist tendency among many of the women who supported the suffrage movement. She described her embarrassment when, as a WSPU member, she had been compelled to share a platform with middle-class suffragettes during the Bury St. Edmunds by-election of 1907 (see Chapter 2) who were 'barnacled with the prejudices of their circle, instinctively hostile to other classes and other races'.[6]

Preoccupation with race was allied to the fear of the re-emergence of a class-conscious socialist movement in the 1880s which threatened to divert the masses away from the 'national interest' – a chauvinistic construct which was widely employed by all European countries in defence of their competing trading and imperial preoccupation. Whereas the 'self-help' ideology of the previous 30 years had reflected the self-confidence of the booming mid-Victorian economy, by the 1880s the challenge to Britain's industrial supremacy from other European countries and America had resulted in a depression of trade and industry. The British Empire acquired a new importance. Now the Empire and its benefits in the form of social imperialism, provided the unifying antidote to the emerging socialist consciousness of the 1880s which threatened to expose the possible class conflict of a declining economy. Social imperialism, a term first used by the Austrian Marxist, Karl Renner, in 1917, was summed up by Disraeli's famous dictum, 'sanitas et imperium' – which meant that the profits from the Empire could be used in part to finance social reform. It was recognised that a mass electorate could not be wooed by self-help alone and that imperial expansion, which of itself demanded popular support if only to provide soldiers to conquer new colonies and defend existing ones from rival imperialisms, could play a key role in winning votes for either of the two parties if it was linked materially to social betterment. The popular culture of the masses both reflected and provided great opportunities to win the expanded electorate for the national, as opposed to the class, cause. Of course, ideology alone could not accomplish this – this is why social imperialism was so important. The writings of all the major imperialist statesmen, Joseph Chamberlain, Cecil Rhodes, Viscount Milner (to name but a few), all made this connection. The point was made earliest and clearest by the Tories, which may help to account for their ascendancy in the latter part of the nineteenth century. The Liberal Party drew lessons from this and adopted a much more aggressively pro-imperialist stance after the fall of Gladstone in 1894.

The renewal of the political consensus in the era of the masses was dependent to a large extent on a renewal of its supportive ideology. The expansion of the British Empire provided the material basis for this. It helped to maintain low prices, especially of food, at a time of economic adversity, thus preventing a drastic drop in real wages for those who had jobs. By providing protected markets it assisted in the maintenance of high profits in certain traditional export industries (the staples) which had lost their competitive edge elsewhere. Those industries thereby, albeit with difficulty and in an altered form, retained a privileged sector of workers who continued to identify their interests with those of the fortunes of their own firm against 'foreign' encroachment. The increased importance of capital exports to the colonies and elsewhere assisted in the creation of further class divisions as a growing army of white-collar clerical workers, many of them women, mushroomed to staff the finance sector of the economy. Finally, there was some truth in the social imperialist argument that the profits from the Empire could be used to finance social reform in Britain. Indeed, the eugenicists argued that such social reform was a necessary condition of the creation of an imperial race. The rejection of many volunteers to fight in the Boer war was an indication that the 'slums and rookeries' of Britain had bred degenerated stock incapable of fulfilling Britain's imperial mission. The real substance of the limited social reforms introduced should not be exaggerated, but for those who were unconvinced by the socialist alternative, they gave continued hope of further improvement within the existing system.

Imperialism, the Labour Movement and Sylvia

Thus it was that imperialism, in an atmosphere of heightened national and racial chauvinism, was able, through the skilful use of popular culture, to employ an ideology and practise with outspokenly racist overtones. Undoubtedly the effect of this was to make it much harder for a comparatively weak socialist movement to gain much ground. Whether or not imperialist and racist ideology penetrated the collective psyche of the labour movement is hard to quantify and is the subject of continued debate. It would be difficult to imagine that it had no impact given its prevalence in every walk of life and the fact that the working-class was the special target of the social imperialists who were quick to spot the dangers of the appeal of socialism at a time when the majority of male workers were enfranchised (1884) and the economy was in the doldrums. The following oft-quoted statement made in 1895 by Cecil Rhodes illustrates perfectly the concerns of the social imperialists:

> I was in the East End of London yesterday and attended a meeting of the unemployed. I listened to the wild speeches which were just a cry for 'bread, bread, bread' and on my way home I pondered over the scene and I became more than ever convinced of the importance of imperialism ... My cherished idea is a solution for the social problem, i.e. in order to save the 40,000,000 inhabitants of the United Kingdom from a bloody civil war, we colonial statesmen must acquire new lands to settle the surplus population, to provide new markets for the goods produced by them in factories and mines. The Empire, as I have always said, is a bread and butter question. If you want to avoid civil war, you must become imperialists.[7]

The attitude of the mainstream labour movement leadership to the Empire was at best silent on the issue and at worst aggressively pro-imperialist. The partition of Africa appeared to escape the notice of the TUC. Its only comment on the enslavement of India was a resolution asking for factory legislation to be introduced in the subcontinent. In 1899 the TUC 'took note' of the Boer War (1899–1901). The 1901 TUC Congress decided to support the war and in 1902 it criticised the government for its 'clumsy handling' of the issue. Such examples, multiplied as the century progressed, were not simply aberrations, but were indicative of an uncritical acceptance of Britain's imperial project.

Sylvia was one of the few on the left who perceived this and was unafraid to comment that 'many of the most powerful trade union leaders are keenly imperialist'.[8] She went on to say that this continuing trend was explained by the fact that these leaders 'are still swayed by current capitalist political influences in international matters'. However, in her view this was a deepseated ideological feature of the British labour movement, not solely confined to the leadership:

> Though the partially awakened rank and file has an instinctive notion that imperialism is something which benefits its masters, it does not realise that imperialism is intimately bound up within its own enslavement to the capitalist system. International solidarity is a sentiment which only attains a sturdy growth amongst those who are fully convinced that capitalism has had its day.

A surprising array of pro-imperialists appeared as opinion formers on the intellectual left. The non-Marxist Fabian Society, formed in 1884 (the 'think-tank' of reformism and later of the Labour right wing), was aggressively pro-imperialist. Its classic text on the subject, *Fabianism and the Empire*, drafted by George Bernard Shaw and published in 1900, could have been written by Cecil Rhodes or Joseph Chamberlain. For the Fabians, the Empire provided the means of accomplishing the social reforms they consistently championed and it led them not in the direction of labour independence, but rather towards political unity with all those who wanted to promote the 'national interest', as opposed to sectional or class interests. Many of them, like H. G.Wells and Shaw himself, were outspokenly racist, and accepted without question the prevalent white supremacist ideology. Hence they were the prime movers behind a project to form a new party of 'National Efficiency'. This was not a political party in the accepted sense, but rather a cross-party 'brains trust' initiated by the Fabians (notably Sidney and Beatrice Webb – social reformers who helped to form the Fabian Society), consisting of leading Liberal and Tory imperialists to discuss the 'aims and methods of Imperial policy'.

Although it might be suspected that the rarefied middle-class intellectualism of the Fabian Society was hardly representative in thought or deed of the labour movement as a whole, the trend it reflected had far-reaching resonances. It was imperialism, particularly social imperialism, rather than the Fabians which gave credence to idea of the 'the national interest' and 'the white man's burden'. This was most sharply expressed in times of war and affected even those with more respectable left-wing credentials than the Fabians. In this connection the Boer War and later the First World War were testing grounds and turning points for the politically conscious section of the labour movement. The leader of the SDF, H. M. Hyndman, opposed the Boer War, as did the ILP (founded in 1893). However, their grounds for opposition had nothing to do with any recognition of the interests of the indigenous black population. Their pro-Boer sentiment was based on their dislike of 'Rand capitalists' who were frequently referred to as 'financial Jews'.

Later, Hyndman and Robert Blatchford (editor of the popular socialist paper, *The Clarion*) became ardent supporters of Britain's 'big navy' programme – the policy of increasing naval expenditure to protect the Empire from rival European imperialism. Hyndman's views did not reflect the majority opinion within his own party, but the fact that he, as its leader, articulated them meant that valuable time and energy was spent waging an internal struggle rather than in conducting an anti-imperialist crusade.

Anti-semitism

Anti-semitism was a powerful current in left circles. In 1904–5 parliament debated the Aliens Immigration Bill introduced by the Balfour government to curb Jewish immigrants fleeing persecution from Tsarist Russia. The ILP issued a pamphlet dealing with this issue.[9] Its author, H. Snell, argued that the government's stance was hypocritical since it had approved of foreign immigration to South Africa, but took a different stand when it came to Britain, thereby reversing a fine tradition that 'has enriched our race with some of the finest blood in the world'. However, Snell drew the line at Jews, rich or poor. In language prefiguring the Nazis, Snell bemoaned the fact that the 'rich Jew' who 'has done his best to besmirch the fair name of England, and to corrupt the sweetness of our national life and character, is to be allowed free entrance to our country, and even to our Parliament'.[10] Although the Jews who had settled in the East End of London, where 'there are whole streets in which the English language is never spoken', clearly did not fit into this category, they were similarly reviled by Snell. The reason – because they were Jews: 'The alien problem in Whitechapel and Stepney is in the main a Jewish problem, a fact that does not make it easier to deal with; let him go where he will the Jew is always an alien, and against his race there exists a prejudice that

corrupts all gentile reasoning.'[11] Given that Snell's pamphlet
was an official ILP publication, one can only presume that he
was reflecting ILP views and was speaking on its behalf when he
concluded that 'as a Labour Party we are not called upon to
contend that all anti-alien feeling is necessarily immoral'.[12]

The attitude of the majority within the leadership of the
British labour movement to imperialism was not that much
worse than the labour movements of other European countries;
the main difference being that the wave of tub-thumping, flag-
waving chauvinism caught independent labour politics in
Britain at its very infancy and gave the older-incorporated political tradition a new lease of life. All over Europe there were great
divisions on the issue, usually dividing hitherto united socialist
parties into pro- and anti-Marxist groupings so that by the time
of the First World War the scene was set for the breakdown of
international class solidarity, expressed in organisational form
through the Second International, into national labour movements all, to varying degrees, supporting the war efforts of their
own country's government.

Black Labour

Even during the most revolutionary phase of the history of the
British labour movement, (c.1910–26), when so many values of
the capitalist system were subjected to scrutiny, racism and
imperialism remained comparatively unchallenged even among
the non-Hyndmanite Marxists. One of the very few debates in
the left press on the issue of racism appeared in *The Call*[13] early
in 1917. This was precipitated by an article on 'Black labour' by
Tom Quelch[14] in which he supported the position of the
Amalgamated Society of Carpenters and Joiners in their opposition to the Labour MP Arthur Henderson's proposal to
introduce black labour into Britain for the purposes of erecting
munitions factories. Apart from the predictable arguments that
this would reduce wages for indigenous white building workers,
Quelch proceeded to denounce the idea in crudely racist tones.
What, he asks sarcastically, can be wrong with 'Fifty thousand
jolly coons, looking picturesque in ill-fitting European clothes
with scarlet bandanas round their heads, boyishly larking as
they toil, shufflin' along in the approved fashion bringing with
them the romance of the wilds coming to Britain?'

One reason, Quelch argued, for opposing black immigration is
the effect it would have on women munitions workers whose

'sex appetites are ... being starved' in the absence of their menfolk and who find it 'impossible to repress natural desires'. These women will be 'delivered into the arms of the vigorous Othellos of Africa'. But to crown his argument, Quelch also employed (spurious) anti-capitalist reasoning. Introducing black labour suited the purposes of the employers because 'race differences aid them in keeping the workers divided. A numerous black population would be of inestimable value to the employers as blacklegs and strike breakers. Ignorant blacks are cheap and unorganised.' The clearly stated basis for Quelch's assertions was the commonly held view that a race problem existed because 'there is a physiological difference between black and white'.

So, was this the Marxist view? According to G. Tchitcherine,[15] Quelch's line was not in accordance with that of the Second International. The International was, Tchitcherine pointed out, opposed to any restriction on the movement of labour, except that of indentured labour. He also took issue with Quelch's view that there was a physiological distinction between the races. The 'setting up of racial distinctions between workers' results in 'the greatest hindrance to the universal development of labour solidarity' and plays into the hands of the capitalists. Quelch replied to this in the following issue[16] in terms more shocking (to us, but perhaps not then), than those in his original article. He did not deal with the policy of the Second International but confined himself to the white supremacist argument. Zulus and Basutos, he wrote 'belong to a different evolutionary epoch' and thus 'their physical and mental characteristics are different from Europeans. It would be better if they all stayed in their own countries – the races cannot mix.'

'Black Scourge in Europe'

Sylvia must have read this correspondence since she worked very closely with the BSP. She was also aware of another racist diatribe emanating from the left. E. D. Morel, ILP member and later Labour MP, wrote an article which was published by the *Herald* in 1920 under the banner headline, 'Black Scourge in Europe'.[17] In it he protested against the French use of black troops in the parts of Germany they occupied after the First World War. It was the fact that black soldiers ('black savages' as he termed them) were being used which so incensed Morel. He asserted that 'primitive African barbarians are perpetuating an abominable outrage upon womanhood, upon the white races and upon civilization' because their unrestrained sexual appetites impelled them to rape white women and to spread syphilis. Although he claimed to have studied this issue in depth, Morel declared that he did not need specific reports to assert the validity of his charges because it was well known that 'the African race is the most developed sexually of any' and the black recruits to the French army come from 'tribes in a primitive state of development ... sexually they are unrestrained and unrestrainable'. Thus the *Herald*, the leading socialist paper of the time and the only daily paper of the left, colluded with Morel's age-old racist stereotypical view of black men as oversexed rapists. Despite the disclaimer in a preface to the article that the *Herald* was 'encouraging colour prejudice', its editorial backed Morel's view on the grounds that 'the manhood of these races' was 'not so advanced in the forms of civilization as ourselves' and warned that if such savages were to be used against Germans 'why not against the workers here or elsewhere'.[18] The *Herald* claimed a great scoop in being the only newspaper to have had the courage to print 'the terrible facts' and proceeded to whip up a campaign to give voice to the 'wave of indignation'[19] which, it was claimed, had swept over England. Despite the continued coverage of the 'Black Troops Terror', only two letters were published on this question, one from a correspondent who saw that misconceived 'facts' about African sexuality are 'one of the greatest sources of race hatred' and 'should never be repeated by any honest man, or honest newspaper'.[20] The other letter, exonerating the *Herald* from any charges of inciting racial hatred, came interestingly from a 'Cardiff negro' who styled himself 'one of the oppressed'. However, it is clear that further letters of critical nature were suppressed. One of these was from Claude McKay, a Jamaican revolutionary poet who lived in London from 1919–21. His letter was printed in the *Workers' Dreadnought*,[21] having been rejected by the *Herald*. McKay strenuously rejected the 'odious' claims made by Morel which he regarded as a further incitement to racial violence against the 'many members of my race, boycotted economically and socially, who have been dumped down on the English docks since the ending of the European War'. The *Herald*'s decision to print such inflammatory material was, according to McKay 'not mitigated by your explanatory editorial'. In his autobiography McKay explains that his motive in writing to George Lansbury as the editor of the *Herald* was to point out 'that it was the duty of his paper as a radical organ to enlighten its readers about the real reason why the English considered coloured troops undesirable in Europe, instead of appealing to illogical emotional prejudices'.[22] He explained that these reasons were to be found in the fact that there was widespread strike action in the Rhineland and that the capitalists were using the race card in order to divert attention:

> The communists had seized important plants. The Junkers were opposing the communists. The social-democratic government was impotent. The French marched in an army … it was not easy to work up and arouse the notorious moral righteousness of the English in favour of the Germans and against the French. Searching for a propaganda issue, the Christian radicals found the coloured troops in the Rhineland. Poor black billy goat.[23]

The publication of McKay's letter in Sylvia's paper led to her suggestion that he should write regularly, from a black perspective, for the *Dreadnought*. McKay thus became Britain's first black reporter.[24] In fact, although this letter led to his first meeting with Sylvia, this was not the first time McKay had written for her paper. A few months before this the *Dreadnought* had published a major front page article by McKay entitled 'Socialism and the Negro'[25] which reported on the work of W. E. B DuBois, the progress of the National Association of the Advancement of Colored People in the United States and the efforts (and difficulties) of the International Workers of the World (the IWW of America, popularly known as the Wobblies), to recruit black people.[26] Despite his criticism of some of the quirkier aspects of Sylvia's politics and personality, McKay, in common with other black radicals and revolutionaries who subsequently made her acquaintance, recognised that she was a fearless and committed revolutionary who understood their cause. As he later wrote:

> in the labor movement she was always jabbing her hat pin into the hides of smug and slack labor leaders. Her weekly might have been called Dread Wasp. And whenever imperialism got drunk and went wild among native peoples, the Pankhurst paper would be on the job.[27]

Indeed, the paper must have been one of the first to notice, let alone criticise, the introduction of the colour bar in South

Africa. Early in 1920, Sylvia wrote a long article on the issue in which she exposed the fact that the majority black population were denied the right to vote or to attend state schools and were subjected to 'pass laws' – the foundation of the apartheid system.[28] Three years later, under the banner headline 'Starvation in South Africa', the entire front page of the paper was devoted to a report of the way in which the indigenous black population was being driven from their own land by white settlers and as a consequence was forced to move to urban areas in search of work.[29]

Her comments on race and empire were not confined to Africa. Indian writers, for example S. N. Ghose, also wrote for the *Workers' Dreadnought*. In 1926 Sylvia published a lengthy tome on India.[30] In it she identified with the growing struggle for Indian self-rule (Swaraj) in its revolutionary civil disobedience phase (1918–22) led by Gandhi who had displaced the more moderate leadership of the Indian National Congress. The British government, fearful of losing the jewel in the imperial crown, attempted to restore their dominance first by coercion (in the form of the Amritsar Massacre 1919) and then by 'consent' via the Government of India Act of 1919. Sylvia sought to expose the 1919 Act as an undemocratic sham – a view unpopular at the time since it was widely perceived as a wise concession smoothing the way to 'responsible' government. Nowadays, however, the balance of received wisdom supports Sylvia's analysis. The Act 'is currently interpreted as being a device to perpetuate British power'.[31] Sylvia was especially critical of the British Labour Party which, by the 1920s, had a strong representation in the House of Commons but did not use it to demand 'representation of the Indian workers and of the poorer Indian peasants'.[32] But the Labour Party, because it was an 'agglomeration of trade unions' was infected with the same imperialist bug. She lamented the demise of Labour's radical and internationalist inheritance. Had it 'been possessed of the sturdy democratic fibre of the Chartists ... it would have offered strenuous opposition to the Government of India Act'[33] and would have gone to the polls pledged to repeal it. Sylvia's book about India has received scant attention and has been treated in a dismissive manner by her biographer, Patricia Romero, but it deserves greater consideration if only for the fact that it is one of the very few anti-imperialist and anti-racist attempts to analyse Indian culture, traditions and history written by an English person. She even attempted to understand, although not to defend, the miserably oppressed status of women in some areas of Indian society. Other feminist writers had shown concern for 'our poor little Indian sisters' (as they were styled in the *Women's Signal*, a feminist journal of the turn of the century)[34] who were forced to undergo child marriages, bride purchase, arranged marriages and other customs which symbolised their inferior status. But as Barbara Caine points out, such consideration was 'often couched in terms which served to belittle or infantilise Indian women'.[35] Whatever else may be said about Sylvia's approach, she did not adopt the haughty superiority of the conquering race.

Anti-fascism and Ethiopia

Sylvia was arguably one of the very few on the left in Britain who understood and saw the dangers of fascism as early as the first years of the 1920s. Her connection with the exiled Italian anarcho-socialist Silvio Corio helped to shape her insight into the first manifestations of fascism in Italy which she followed closely. She regarded Mussolini's March on Rome in 1922 as marking 'the final collapse of the post war revolutionary movement'.[36] Such comment was not made only with the wisdom of hindsight. She wrote a long article, 'The truth about the fascisti',[37] at the time (1922) in which she roundly castigated the *Daily Herald* for its 'unexampled treachery' in expressing admiration for Mussolini's 'bloodless revolution'. Mussolini was widely regarded as Italy's saviour from communism. She was similarly contemptuous of the ILP publication the *Socialist Review* for publishing a eulogy of Mussolini and fascism by an Italian living in London. The article, she said, was 'a tissue of lies from start to finish'.[38]

Sylvia was one of the few voices on the left, outside of the Communist Party, who exposed the terrorist methods of the fascisti and revealed their links with big business in an effort to defeat the workers. Her analysis of fascism, notwithstanding her later break with communism, remained very similar to that of the Italian communist leader, Palmiro Togliatti.[39] In seeking to explain why she had spoken at a protest meeting 'against dictatorship whether Bolshevik or Fascist' she was at pains to point out that she disagreed with the title of the meeting and offered the following analysis of fascism:

What is fascism? It is the organisation of extra-governmental violence to prevent the capitalist government of society from being superseded by a new and more advanced form of social organisation ... Fascism ... is a wholly military manifestation. It soon over-rides all civil government and crushes out all democratic practices. [It] is essentially a manifestation of capitalism having felt danger and revenging itself for having been made to fear for its existence.[40]

She was appalled by the murder in 1923 of the Italian socialist deputy, Giacomo Matteotti, at the hands of the fascists. When, in 1932, she discovered that his widow, Velia, and her children were in danger, she formed the Women's International Matteotti Committee to draw attention to their plight and campaigned for their removal to Britain. She obtained the signatures of many prominent people on a petition for the Matteotti cause. It is interesting to note, however, that George Bernard Shaw refused to sign since he supported the idea of a fascist Corporate State.

From 1923 to 1945 Sylvia did everything possible to assist the opponents and victims of fascism. She was involved with refugee organisations, particularly those seeking to aid Jews fleeing from persecution. She helped find jobs and accommodation for them.

The second half of Sylvia's life, from 1935 to her death in 1960 was devoted to the cause of the liberation of Ethiopia. Her decision to take up the cause of a little-known (in England) African country might have seemed odd to contemporaries and has been largely ignored by British historians. However, it was much appreciated by black activists in Africa, the West Indies, Britain and America and can only be understood in the context of her anti-racism and anti-imperialism which had already surfaced early in the century. This was allied to her understanding of the dangers of fascism in general and Italian fascism in particular. Thus, when Italy invaded Ethiopia in 1935, Sylvia embarked on a course which was to draw these strands of her thought and activity into a campaign which was to absorb her for the remainder of her life. In May 1936 she launched the first edition of the *New Times and Ethiopia News (NT&EN)*, a weekly paper whose aims were to champion the cause of Ethiopia, to combat fascist propaganda, to campaign for British aid and to step up and maintain the economic sanctions imposed on Italy by the League of Nations. The first issue went to press on the very day that Italian troops entered Addis Ababa. The paper reached a circulation of 10,000 by the end of the year, and at its height it sold 40,000 copies weekly. This included an extensive circulation throughout West Africa and the West Indies where 'it was widely quoted in the emerging African nationalist press'.[41] The paper was also published (occasionally) in Amharic and clandestinely distributed in Ethiopia. It remained in circulation for 20 years.

Sylvia's decision to devote 25 years of her life to the Ethiopian cause has been much misunderstood. Romero regards her motivation as being predicated upon her idolisation of the Emperor, Haile Selassie, who became for her 'a hero and father figure to whom she would be loyal for the rest of her life'.[42] Surprisingly this view is also shared by Winslow, a much more sympathetic biographer,[43] who asserts (incorrectly) that Sylvia 'basked in Selassie's company as his confidante and political adviser' from 1935 until her death in 1960 and that the incongruity of her position as a socialist and republican now defending an Emperor is partly to be explained by his role as 'another father figure' in her life. Apart from the somewhat insulting and unproven nature of such psychologistic interpretations, it hardly accords with the facts. Sylvia had not met the Emperor when she decided to take up the Ethiopian cause. A more tenable view, and one which accords with her understanding of the dynamics of racism, is that given by her son Richard Pankhurst,[44] who worked closely with her, in later years, on the Ethiopian cause. He advances the view that Sylvia's motivation was primarily one of anti-fascism but with the important qualification that the left in Britain was less inclined to take up the cause of Ethiopia because it was an African country and hence found Spain a more acceptable anti-fascist cause. This is not a hindsight interpretation. Sylvia regarded fascist aggression as having commenced in Ethiopia and spread to Spain with Italy 'supplying its Fascist ally with aeroplanes, and ... the German ally ... supplying cash.'[45] However, she wrote, 'People stood by while Ethiopia was vanquished: this is only Africa; this is not a White Man's country. They listened to the Italian propaganda; these are the primitives, their customs are barbarous'.

Indeed, as Ron Ramdin[46] points out, Pan-Africanists like George Padmore[47] were critical of the terms on which the British left supported the Republican cause in Spain. Padmore was concerned by the implicit racism of the left's frequent con-

demnation of the use of Moorish troops by Franco. This is not
to say that Padmore or Sylvia herself considered that the
Spanish cause was unimportant – far from it. Reports on the
Spanish Civil War appeared each week in the *NT&EN* from 1936
onwards with headlines urging that 'it must be saved'. She considered Spain and Ethiopia to be part of a single common
struggle against fascism.[48]

However, Sylvia's decision to concentrate her energies on
Ethiopia was taken because it would otherwise have been
largely ignored. Ethiopia was very significant for black people
worldwide. It was, until 1935, the only independent country in
Africa – the only African country to have escaped from the domination of European imperialism. As such it was a beacon in the
anti-colonial struggle. Its long-established culture and traditions, untrammelled by the yoke of white domination, were
and still are highly regarded as an expression of black pride and
identity. Ethiopia was, according to Ras Makonnen, the 'black
man's last citadel'.[49] Pride in Ethiopia was not unique to West
Indian Ras Tafaris who revered Haile Selassie as the living God.
This was clearly shown when, as a response to the Italian invasion, mass protests were organised in almost all Britain's West
Indian colonies,[50] provoking fear in the British Colonial Office
that 'native unrest' would be stirred in colonial Africa. Tellingly,
Hesketh Bell, a former governor of Uganda, expressed the issue
thus:

> The fact that the coloured inhabitants of a distant West
> Indian island, remembering their African ancestry, should
> appear to feel so deeply this attack by a white power on the
> only remaining negro nation shows how widely spread and
> vigorous can be the influences of race and colour. While the
> rise of feeling of racial antagonism in the West Indies is
> unfortunate, the development of such an attitude among the
> teeming population of our vast African territories would be a
> misfortune of the first magnitude.[51]

The Colonial Secretary in Sierra Leone, H. R. R. Blood, was
similarly concerned about the new mood among Africans of the
West Coast as a result of the Italo-Ethiopian conflict and the
fact that British inaction was seen as a breach of faith, stimulat-
ing protest activity from the Youth League established by
Wallace Johnson in 1938. Clearly the *NT&EN* was having an
influence on radical and nationalist opinion, since in 1939

Blood listed the paper as one of those to be banned in Sierra Leone under an 'Undesirable Literature Bill'. Despite protests from Sylvia and others, the paper was proscribed.

Ethiopia's role in galvanising 'the influences of race and colour' (Hesketh Bell), was plainly apparent in the black communities of Britain and the USA. In anticipation of the Italian invasion the International African Friends of Abyssinia (IAFA) was formed in 1935. Although this was a short lived organisation it involved many prominent black activists including Jomo Kenyatta, C. L. R. James, Amy Ashwood Garvey (ex-wife of Marcus Garvey) and George Padmore. Esedebe[52] estimates that after the invasion, 12 separate Ethiopian defence committees were formed in Britain. Most of them were short lived, none played such a such an important role as the IAFA and its successor organisation, and none was as long-lived as the *NT&EN*.

It is clear that Sylvia not only had an understanding of the significance of Ethiopia for black people, but that she also understood the importance of reasserting African values against the imperialist counter-culture. As a result she consistently supported efforts to challenge the white notion of black racial inferiority. The paper ran a regular column entitled 'Africa for the Africans' which was very popular and was often reprinted together with many other *NT&EN* articles in such influential African papers as the *Comet* and the *West African Pilot*. Thus it was that although her paper was devoted to championing the Ethiopian cause and combatting fascist propaganda, it was also a force within the emerging African nationalist movement, which, according to Asante,[53] was the biggest single force in awakening racial and political consciousness in West Africa and the diaspora. Sylvia's paper also gave space to anti-racist initiatives. As early as 1936 it carried an article on 'African education'[54] which argued that 'Historical books on Africa ought to be written by Africans and ought to aim at developing the "national ego" of the African instead of dwelling on intertribal wars'. Later in the same year the paper published a letter from Marcus Garvey, the black American leader, protesting against films like *Sanders of the River*, *Emperor Jones* and *Green Pastures* which, according to Garvey, were 'calculated to create prejudice against the Negro Race'.[55] Many years later, in correspondence with another black American leader and theoretician, the communist W. E. B. DuBois, Sylvia expressed her dislike of the term 'negro' since she regarded it as a term foisted on black people first by the British and then by

Americans. She wrote to him explaining that 'Ethiopia does not recognise the term "negro" as applied to the whole African people, and regards it as a rather Americanised version of the matter. The term African is greatly preferred, or even the term "Ethiopian" as the ancients used.'[56] She went on to say, in a remarkably astute prefiguring of much later debates in the anti-racist movement, that she herself preferred the use of the term 'Afro-American' for black Americans. DuBois agreed with her that the term 'negro' was not perfect and that it was the 'result of long controversy and misunderstanding'. None the less, he went on to say that 'The one point we want to emphasise is that the darker peoples of Africa and the Americas who are descended from African slaves, belong to a group that is not only unified by descent but by its relation to the white European world.'[57]

Although *NT&EN* was primarily a campaigning paper, it also published articles of a more theoretical kind written by black academics and political leaders, dealing with the nature of imperialism and racism. One of the most important of these contributions was a remarkable two-part article entitled 'The influence of colonialism and racial conflicts on the development and maintenance of free societies' written by Dr A. K. Busia, Professor of Sociology at the University College of the Gold Coast.[58] This was a penetrating analysis of imperialism which prefigured many of today's academic debates on colonial imperatives. Dr Busia, while anticipating and dealing with the counter-arguments, displayed a much clearer insight than many of today's 'experts'.

Richard Pankhurst, Professor of Ethiopian Studies at the University of Addis Ababa, has documented the remarkable role played by the *NT&EN* in maintaining public awareness of the Ethiopian struggle for independence and beyond.[59] The contribution made by the paper was noted by many black people, and can be summarised by Ras Makonnen who said of it that it: 'continued for many years to be the most authorative single source on the Ethiopian question. In particular it seldom failed to document the many pro-Ethiopian meetings in England and to note black participation in them.'[60] For black activists like Makonnen, Haile Selassie was the leader of Ethiopia's anti-fascist liberation struggle. In 1936, the Emperor left Ethiopia with his family in order to plead the cause of his country to the League of Nations in Geneva. He took up residence in England and when he arrived in London, Sylvia was part of the group which went to meet him. Thereafter she visited him on many occasions. In this context we must note that the criticism made of Sylvia's friendship with the Emperor did not find an echo with radical black activists of her time. In contrast to the white left, who wrote Haile Selassie off as a feudal dictator, the black left,[61] despite sharing many similar misgivings about the Emperor's politics, did not allow this to cloud their judgement as to the positive role he played during this period.[62] This also meant that Sylvia's friendship with the Emperor was seen by black radicals as an act of international solidarity.[63] None the less, Sylvia was not starry eyed. Richard Pankhurst reports that at their first meeting 'she told him frankly as a republican that she supported him not because he was an emperor, but because she believed that his cause, the cause of Ethiopia, was a just one'.[64]

Apart from acknowledging that Sylvia's decision to devote herself to this issue was a product of her anti-racism, it is not the purpose of this chapter to deal in any depth with the vicissitudes of the Ethiopian struggle. Her involvement in that struggle brought her into contact with a remarkable group of Pan-Africanists resident as exiles in London. These included Ras Makonnen, C. L. R. James, Jomo Kenyatta, I. T. A. Wallace Johnson and George Padmore. In 1937 Padmore and Wallace Johnson founded the International African Service Bureau (IASB) [65] The IASB itself was a product of the Ethiopian solidarity movement, being an outgrowth of IAFA. The IASB lasted for seven years, until 1944. It was the longest surviving of all the Pan-African associations formed during this period. It merged, in 1944, with the Pan-African Federation, the organisation which was largely responsible for the convening of the 1945 Pan-African Congress. Thus in a very real sense, Ethiopia was the theoretical and practical catalyst for the further development of the anti-racist and anti-colonial struggle.[66] The motto of the IASB was 'educate, co-operate, emancipate – neutral in nothing affecting the African people'. Sylvia was a member of the IASB committee of associates for a time – the only woman among six men, who included Victor Gollancz (publisher and founder of the Left Book Club) and the lawyer, D. N. Pritt. The first issue of the IASB monthly journal, *International African Opinion,* singled out the Ethiopian struggle as the catalyst which has 'awakened black political consciousness'. It argued that Ethiopia had shown that 'all Negroes everywhere are beginning to see the necessity for international organisation and the uni-

fication of their scattered efforts'.[67] Sylvia has left little record of
her activity with this group. However, we must assume, in the
light of her anti-fascist stance, which was redoubled with the
approach of the Second World War, that she must have had
some difficulty with the IASB's refusal to support the war
against Nazi Germany, which the IASB characterised as an
'imperialist war' from which Africans should remain aloof. This
position was summarised in the title of an IASB pamphlet published in 1938, *Europe's Difficulty is Africa's Opportunity*.

Sylvia was already involved in popular front anti-fascist, anti-
militarist activity. She had become treasurer of the International
Women's World Committee against War and Fascism – an
organisation founded in Paris in 1934 which sought to put pressure on the League of Nations and the major powers to
maintain collective security in order to stem fascist aggression.
Unlike the British Labour Party, which resolutely refused to participate in any popular front initiatives lest it be tainted with
the bogey of communism, this international women's organisation did not allow such sectarian considerations to over-ride the
importance of the cause it espoused. Hence its founding conference consisted of a broad array of communist and
non-communist women. Its British sponsors included many
famous names such as Vera Brittain, Ellen Wilkinson, Charlotte
Despard and, of course, Sylvia. She regarded Chamberlain's pact
with Hitler at Munich as 'the basest day in British history'.[68]
Sylvia was not a pacifist – the failure of diplomacy led her and
many others to the inevitable conclusion that the Nazi menace
could only be stopped by force. Hence, when war started in
1939, she formed and became the secretary of the Women's
War Emergency Council, a body which, while supporting the
war, agitated to ensure that 'equality of sacrifice' was a reality.

However, work on Ethiopia took precedence, and the
Women's War Emergency Council was short lived. When, in
1940, Italy declared war on Britain, Sylvia campaigned to ensure
that the British government accorded Ethiopia the status of an
ally. Although she eventually managed to get the BBC to play
the Ethiopian national anthem along with those of all the other
allies, it was clear that the British government did not intend to
restore full independence to Ethiopia after it had been liberated
from Italy by the Allies in 1941. Instead it was classed as occupied enemy territory and a large part of it remained under
British occupation. Hence the *NT&EN* acquired a new role, 'that
of working for the liberation of Ethiopia from its liberators'.[69]

Whilst the first and second Anglo-Ethiopian Agreements, which the Ethiopian government was forced to sign in 1942 and 1944 respectively, formally recognised Ethiopian independence, Britain remained in control of large parts of the country. Furthermore, in classic divide-and-rule formula, Britain insisted that Eritrea and the Ogaden, despite their strong wishes to the contrary, remained separated from Ethiopia. Hence the cause of Ethiopia was still pressing and Sylvia remained committed to it until she died.

Given that she had become well known and greatly respected in African circles, one can only presume that she was not present at the Fifth Pan-African Congress held in Manchester in 1945 because she had been in Ethiopia in 1944–45 and through the *NT&EN* had organised a conference in April 1945 to galvanise opposition to the second Anglo-Ethiopian Agreement. One of the speakers at the Ethiopia conference, indeed the mover of the main resolution, was Jomo Kenyatta of Kenya who was one of the organisers of the 1945 Pan-African Congress held in October. Clearly Sylvia must have known about the Manchester Congress and was in the country at the time. The congress was undoubtedly the most important of the Pan-African Congresses held to date 'representing the zenith of the the Pan-African movement'[70] in that its 90 participants came not as individuals, as in previous congresses, but as delegates from their organisations. Although African countries were well represented, there were no delegates from Ethiopia. Whatever the reason for Sylvia's non-attendance at this important event, it did not betoken any lessening of the links between her and the Pan-African movement. When in 1946 *NT&EN* organised another meeting to protest against the Labour government's annexationist plans for the Ogaden, the speakers included Ras Makonnen and Peter Abrahams (from the African National Congress of South Africa), both of whom played a major role in the Pan-African movement. Later in the year, on the eve of the international conference of foreign ministers called to discuss the future of Italy's former African colonies, Sylvia convened an Ethiopian solidarity conference at Caxton Hall, London. George Padmore, the celebrated Pan-Africanist and prime mover of the 1945 Conference, was one of the speakers.

It was not until 1950 that the United Nations finally decided that Eritrea could be federated with Ethiopia, thus leaving British occupation of a large part of the country as the only remaining issue for the independence movement. This was resolved in 1954 when Britain finally withdrew from the 'Reserved Area', although in the meantime, the danger of the restoration of Italian rule had arisen to frustrate the hopes of the Ethiopians. For almost 20 years *NT&EN* had campaigned relentlessly, through its columns and through its capacity to mobilise, for the restoration of Ethiopian independence, first against the Italians and then against the British. By 1954, however, the battle had been won. For the *NT&EN* this was a signal that 'its mission was thus drawing to a close'.[71] In a letter to Teresa Billington Greig, Sylvia wrote that she regarded the campaign to achieve Ethiopian independence as her greatest achievement.

The last issue of the paper appeared in 1954. It was succeeded by the *Ethiopia Observer* and later the *Journal of Ethiopian Studies*, the latter co-edited by Richard Pankhurst and his wife, Rita. In 1956, aged 74, Sylvia accepted an invitation issued by the Ethiopian government to live there. She was an honoured guest – her work in supporting Ethiopian independence was well known: a street in Addis Ababa had been named after her and she had been presented with two medals, the Queen of Sheba medal and the Patriot's medal. She died in Ethiopia in 1960 at the age of 78 and was given a state funeral, and, although a life long agnostic, she was buried in the graveyard reserved for Ethiopian patriots in the principal Addis Ababa Cathedral.

Accolades to Sylvia on her death show that although her work on Ethiopia, informed as it was by anti-racism and anti-imperialism, passed largely unnoticed in Britain, it was widely appreciated by black people in Ethiopia, in Africa generally and in the diaspora. DuBois, arguably one of the most important black leaders of his day, expressed the view of black radicals in the following tribute he paid to Sylvia following her death:

> I realised ... that the great work of Sylvia Pankhurst was to introduce black Ethiopia to white England, to give the martyred Emperor of Ethiopia a place of refuge during his exile and to make the British people realise that black folks had more and more to be recognised as human beings with the rights of women and men.[72]

7

Assessment

Ever since some of the myths about women's suffrage history
have been exposed by radical historians, Sylvia Pankhurst has
emerged as something of an icon for socialist feminists. Her
attempts to navigate a course linking women's militancy and
class politics have struck a chord between us 'second-wave feminists' of 1960s vintage who have been engaged, albeit in altered
circumstances, on a similar project in which similar difficulties
have been encountered. The attempt to link the 'separate
spheres' of the women's movement and the labour movement
have been beset from time to time by the lack of vision of sep-
aratist feminists on the one hand and the patriarchal myopia of
the labour movement on the other – precisely the problems she
encountered.

However, icon status is something that should not be wished
on anyone – it is far too great a responsibility to bear and in any
case makes for the same bad history which in the past has presumed that the study of kings or queens encapsulates the age in
which they live. Naturally it would be incorrect, undesirable
and downright daft to presume that Sylvia Pankhurst, or any
individual, was a repository of truth, wisdom and unerring
political judgement. Throughout her long life she espoused
many causes – not all of them dealt with in this book – in some
of which she undoubtedly made a major contribution. Until
now only her suffrage work has been fully appreciated, but it is
clear that she played an important, albeit sometimes quixotic,
role in at least two other spheres: the early communist movement and the anti-racist and anti-fascist movement. Both these
arenas were ones in which women's inclusion was noted by its
exceptionalism. It is not simply a case of rescuing a woman who
has been 'hidden from history' in respect of Sylvia's work in the
male world of left politics. What emerges clearly is that Sylvia
was not a 'bit player' – she was an initiator and a leader in her
own right.

Sylvia, like all of us, was a product of her times, but at the
same time she was avant-garde and hence not part of the main-

stream. She was not the only socialist feminist of her age, nor the only anti-fascist. There are two ways in which it is possible to assess her contribution. One involves a judgement of whether she was right or wrong and the other is less of a personal approach and involves an assessment of the labour and women's movements' responsiveness to the kind of issues in which she was involved. This book has adopted the second approach. The first method, the one used by most biographers, is the one which objectifies the individual and almost by definition involves the author's subjective judgement of that individual's personal or political qualities. If you like them and their politics you pick out all the good bits and regard anything else as an aberration. In the case of Sylvia there would be many aberrations – she was individualistic, inconsistent politically, often unable to work collectively and probably somewhat eccentric. Her passion for Ethiopia may well have clouded her judgement of its Emperor in the post-fascist period. Such an approach may, with some justification, point to a lack of consistency in her political approach, which followed a very bumpy and unpredictable path throughout her life as she went from creative art to feminism to socialist feminism to communism to left sectarianism to reformism (of sorts). Thus communists will like some parts of her, Trotskyists will like others and so on through to feminists, anti-racists and perhaps even monarchists. Almost everyone can find something to admire in her, although very few will identify or like the entire opus. Perhaps this is why only one full biography of Sylvia has been published[1] and the only way that its author has been able to impose a consistent theme to knit all the strands of her life together is by seeking father-deprivation as a central core to explain it all.

The fact that the issue-based approach has been adopted in this book is not solely because Sylvia is, for the reasons given above, such a difficult subject. Rather it is because the issues themselves are so important and that an assessment of political correctness of an individual espousing them lets us off the hook of making a more important judgement – that of the movements' responsiveness (or otherwise) to the issues. It is not, therefore, a matter of whether Sylvia got it all right or all wrong, but whether the movements she sought to influence did. In this sense, this book uses Sylvia as a litmus test for assessing the labour and women's movement. The objection to this may be twofold: first that her style of work may well have detracted support, and second that other individuals espoused her causes and may thus be better exemplars of them. Clearly the first objection is meaningful and some account of it has been taken. In countering the second objection, however, the claim for Sylvia as the chosen exemplar must be substantiated. Herein lies the assessment of her contribution.

Whilst there were undoubtedly other individuals who took up some or all of the three major issues discussed in this book, there was no one else who espoused them all in the high-profile way in which she did, and more important there was no woman (as far as I can tell to date) who made a major contribution to all three in what may be called leadership terms. Her suffrage activity in the East End was certainly not the only example of socialist feminist activity among working-class women, although it was the only example of a women from the 'militant' WSPU tradition engaging in this type of work. She was by no means the only feminist who sought a link with organised labour, although she was one of the very few who established that link through the socialist rank and file and the emerging revolutionary movement. She was not the only woman to be involved in the formation of the Communist Party, although (as is argued in Chapter 5) she made a unique contribution to publicising and winning support for the Russian Revolution and the Third International. She was certainly the only woman to edit and run a weekly paper of any kind for a lengthy period (ten years), let alone one which gave expression to socialism, feminism and anti-racism, and she was the first person to employ a black journalist. She was not the only woman to challenge the accepted norms of family life and openly have a child 'out of wedlock', but she made an early and important contribution to the campaign for maternity benefits which was predicated on the assumption that not all mothers had husbands. Obviously she was not the only anti-fascist in Britain, although she was one of the first to expose the dangers of fascism and reveal the real nature of Mussolini's populism. She was, in addition, one of the very few among the white left to make the link between fascism and racism and was, as far as my research shows, virtually alone among white politicians in this country, in her stance, from at least the 1920s, against racism and imperialism. So although not unique in every particular, except perhaps the last, she was certainly unique in her espousal of all three issues mentioned. If we add to this the fact that she had 'political flair' (as Walter Holmes put it) and tireless organising capacity, it can be appreciated that her contribution to the causes she embraced was never undertaken quietly and never without effect. So there has been good reason for taking Sylvia Pankhurst as both subject and object. Her contribution overall has been underestimated, but equally the labour and women's movements' contribution to some of Sylvia's 'causes' has to be judged in a more critical light.

There is, however, one other strand of her life and work which must also be considered. Although Sylvia pre-dates the later link made by feminists between the personal and the political, she herself lived her politics, especially her feminism. Throughout the ebb and flow of her varied political career, she retained a deep commitment to women's liberation. This was not just a theoretical position. Her own life was testimony to its living meaning. In 1927, at the age of 45, she shocked British society by giving birth to her son, Richard, out of wedlock. Although the baby's father, Silvio Corio, was a doting one, the two never married, much to the shock and chagrin of Emmeline and Christabel Pankhurst. It is difficult to realise now, over 70 years later, quite how fearless she was in rejecting the accepted moral code, especially since she did so as a matter of principle and refused to reveal the identity of the father to scandal-mongering journalists. Eight years later, in an article specially written for the *Daily Mirror*[2] about her decision 'to become a mother without legal marriage', which had 'shocked the world', Sylvia declared in a banner headline 'I have **no** regrets' – 'I always hated Mrs Grundy'. This chance comment is a real clue to Sylvia's character – whatever the cause she was unafraid to tilt at the windmill of convention. This was a constant theme throughout her life and probably accounts for the strong feelings, of a positive or negative nature, which she excited in others, including those in her own family. Of course, the breach between her and her mother and elder sister was, in origin, political and was exacerbated by Emmeline and Christabel's alarming shift to the right. However, the fact that her relations barely spoke to her again after 1914 was also due to the fact that Sylvia adopted a lifestyle of which they profoundly disapproved. She cared little about clothes or appearance, she had chosen to live with the working class in one of the poorest areas of Britain[3] and to cap it all she was an unmarried mother whose house was filled with black radical exiles, Jewish refugees, Ethiopian students and many others. Without deliberation on her part, Sylvia's lifestyle was, perforce, unconventional even by today's standards. How much more did it appear so in Edwardian England?

The British labour movement was far more conventional. Its espousal of such seemingly radical departures as feminism and anti-racism is still unsettled. In Sylvia's day there was less pressure on the labour movement, despite the strong pre-1914 women's movement, to change its ideological stance on these issues and in any case, as we have noted, the labour-suffrage alliance had been placed under considerable strain by the anti-labour policies of the WSPU. After the war, the pressure on the leadership of the labour movement was even less. Winning the vote seemed to have silenced the collective voice of women and the dominant values reasserting women's primary domestic role were championed as much by trade unionists as by the establishment. Racist ideas were, as we have seen, deeply ingrained in mainstream labour movement thought, including sections of the left. To suggest that the movement was found wanting in this regard is a simple truism. However, the commonly accepted view that it is historicist moralism to impose our own concerns on a labour movement which knew no different, begs a very important question. Is it really the case that 50 and more years ago no one understood the nature of racism and imperialism? The previous chapter of this book has indicated that not only Sylvia, but black radicals in the colonies, in this country and the USA had a sophisticated understanding of the link between race and empire. The fact that the labour movement and the white left, with a few notable exceptions, ignored such literature and campaigning, serves only to show how deeply the dominant culture of the imperial motherland had entrenched itself. The fact that Sylvia was one of the few among the white left who grasped the link between race and empire serves only to highlight the power of the dominant ideology's stranglehold on the labour movement. This is not a moral judgment, but a matter of historical fact which can only be redressed if it is acknowledged.

Sylvia Pankhurst did acknowledge it and spent her whole life actively seeking, in word and deed, to redress the strangulating divisiveness of racism and sexism.

Notes

All books published in London unless otherwise specified.

Introduction

1. E. Sylvia Pankhurst, *The Suffragette Movement*, Virago, 1977, p. 608.
2. Among the most useful are the following: Pankhurst, *The Suffragette Movement*; Jill Liddington and Jill Norris, *With One Hand Tied Behind Us*, Virago, 1978; Marion Ramelson, *The Petticoat Rebellion*, Lawrence and Wishart, 1972; Susan Kent, *Sex and Suffrage in Britain 1860–1914*, Princeton University Press, 1987; Jane Rendall (ed.), *Equal or Different: Women's Politics 1800–1914*, Basil Blackwell, 1987; Les Garner, *Stepping Stones to Women's Liberty*, Heinemann, 1984.
3. Hereinafter I shall refer to her as Sylvia. It is usual to refer to historical subjects by their surnames, but in this case it is confusing since the Pankhurst name was shared by Sylvia's equally famous mother and sister. I am aware that the use of her first name only implies a level of familiarity and a certain lack of respect which is rarely employed when dealing with male subjects, but the use of her initials, ESP (Estelle Sylvia Pankhurst), might be confusing!
4. The only full-scale biography of Sylvia Pankhurst was published in 1987 by Patricia Romero: *E. Sylvia Pankhurst: Portrait of a Radical*, Yale University Press.
5. The nickname 'suffragette' was bestowed on the WSPU by the *Daily Mail* – it was readily accepted by that organisation since it served to distinguish it from the older suffrage societies (and supporters of women's suffrage in general) who were known as suffragists.
6. See in particular the work of Liddington and Norris, *With One Hand Tied*.

7. Barbara Winslow, *Sylvia Pankhurst: Sexual Politics and Political Activism*, UCL Press, 1996. Winslow deals with Sylvia's most revolutionary years. She does not claim to have written a full-scale biography and hence the fact that the detailed narrative stops in 1924 is in no sense a criticism of her offering.

Chapter 1

1. See Barbara Taylor, *Eve and the New Jerusalem*, Virago, 1991 and R. and E. Frow (eds), *Political Women*, Pluto Press, 1989.
2. This was the practice whereby the Liberal Party, since the Second Reform Act in 1867, had encouraged working men in predominantly working-class constituencies to stand as Liberal candidates in elections. The 1867 Act had enfranchised better paid working men – those who in shorthand terms were labelled the 'labour aristocracy'.
3. Quoted in Sarah Boston, *Women Workers and the Trade Unions*, Davis-Poynter, 1980, p. 16.
4. See Chapter 2.
5. *The Syndicalist* was the organ of the Syndicalist Education League. It appeared regularly for two years from 1912 to 1914. It was the successor to *The Syndicalist Railwayman*, founded by Guy Bowman and edited by Charles Watkins. I wish to record my grateful thanks to John Hammond, trade union activist (then Public Service, Tax and Commerce Union (PTC) now Public and Commercial Services Union (PCS)) and bibliophile, who presented me with a facsimile edition of this rare journal (Spokesman Books 1975). John was a former student who gained a distinction on the Certificate in Higher Education in Labour and Trade Union Studies, a course then taught at South Bank University (now at the University of North London). John Hammond tragically died in his prime of life in 1997. He was a deeply committed, patient, wise and kind man.
6. *The Syndicalist*, December 1913.
7. *The Syndicalist*, January 1914. The only reference to the East London Federation of Suffragettes was a sympathetic report of the 'No Vote No Rent' campaign.

8. *The Great Scourge and How to End It* (E. Pankhurst, 1913) concerned itself with the threat to the survival of the British 'race' due to what Christabel regarded as the pestilence of sexually transmitted diseases. Her solution was to advocate chastity for men!

9. *The Syndicalist*, January 1914.

10. The SDF changed its name twice – in 1909 to the Social Democratic Party, and in 1911 to the British Socialist Party.

11. Belfort Bax joined Morris, Eleanor Marx, Edward Aveling and others when they broke away from the SDF in late 1884 to form the Socialist League.

12. E. Belfort Bax, *The Fraud of Feminism*, Grant Richards, 1913, p. 23.

13. Ibid., p. 31.

14. Ibid., p. 17.

15. SDF Conference Report, 1908, quoted in Christine Collette, *For Labour and for Women*, Manchester University Press, 1989.

16. Editorial, *Justice*, 16 March 1912.

17. 'Crisis' column, *Justice*, 23 March 1912.

18. *Justice*, 30 March 1912.

19. 'Social democracy and votes for women 1', *Justice*, 27 July 1912.

20. 'Social democracy and votes for women 2', *Justice*, 3 August 1912.

21. *Votes for Women*, 19 January 1912.

22. *Justice*, 31 August 1912.

23. Termed 'Census re Working Women Householders'. Each ILP branch was asked to go through the voting lists for municipal elections to find 'particulars of the number of women voters and the proportion of working women among them' (ILP National Administrative Council minutes, 26 January 1905. ILP collection, British Library of Economic and Political Science, London).

24. Jill Liddington is probably correct in her estimation that the 'the figures were of doubtful worth' (*Liddington, The Life and Times of a Respectable Rebel: Selina Cooper 1864–1946*, Virago, 1984, p. 145).

25. *The Labour Leader*, 11 January 1907.

26. Published in *The Labour Leader*, 1 February 1907.

27. Ramsay MacDonald in *The Labour Leader*, 12 April 1907.

28. 'Political equality campaign', article by James Myles (ILP London Divisional Organiser), 12 January 1912.
29. Ibid.
30. Sylvia Pankhurst, *The Suffragette Movement*.
31. Described by Liddington and Norris as 'a Liberal at heart'; *With One Hand Tied*, p. 155.
32. MPs were not paid by the state until 1911.
33. Quoted in Liddington and Norris, *With One Hand Tied*, p. 157.
34. For a full account of the activities of the long-neglected radical suffragists see Liddington and Norris, ibid., and Liddington's biography of Selina Cooper, *Life and Times*.

Chapter 2

1. Liddington, *Life and Times*, p. 220. Liddington correctly points out that this development has been neglected by suffrage historians. Aside from the suffrage, the alliance had other important implications, not least of which was the weakening of lib-labism.
2. Sylvia Pankhurst, *The Suffragette Movement*, p. 167. She is here paraphrasing the words of Isabella Ford, the long-standing socialist and suffragist who was elected to the ILP executive in 1903
3. Ibid.
4. Emmeline Pankhurst, *My Own Story*, Virago, 1979.
5. Christabel Pankhurst, *Unshackled – the Story of How We Won the Vote*, Hutchinson, 1959, p. 32.
6. Liddington, *Life and Times*, p. 140.
7. This is the dominant theme of Patricia Romero's view of Sylvia's activities in the WSPU in *E. Sylvia Pankhurst*.
8. Christabel Pankhurst, *Unshackled*, p. 44.
9. See June Hannam's biography, *Isabella Ford*, Basil Blackwell, 1989.
10. Unpublished handwritten manuscript, 'Autobiographical notes', 1937. From the E. Sylvia Pankhurst papers (hereafter PP) no. 67, International Institute of Social History, Amsterdam.
11. Ibid.
12. Brian Harrison, *Separate Spheres – the Opposition to Women's Suffrage in Britain*, Croom Helm, 1978.

13.   For a fuller analysis of the labour movement's attitude to women's suffrage see Chapter 1.
14.   *The Labour Leader*, 15 August 1904.
15.   *The Labour Leader*, 9 September 1904.
16.   Letter to the *Co-operative News*, 10 December 1904, Gertrude Tuckwell collection TUC Library, London.
17.   Published as 'A Verbatim Report on December 3rd 1907 – Sex Equality (T. B. Greig) versus Adult Suffrage (M. Bondfield)', Women's Freedom League, 1909.
18.   Ibid.
19.   Ibid.
20.   Ibid.
21.   Ibid.
22.   Ibid. At the end of the debate the motion, 'that the immediate granting of the Parliamentary franchise to women on the same terms as it is or may be granted to men is the speediest and most practical way to real democracy', was carried by 171 votes in favour to 139 against.
23.   Sylvia Pankhurst, *The Suffragette Movement*, p. 203.
24.   In 1906 Charles Dilke, a Liberal MP, introduced an Adult Suffrage Bill. It was opposed by the women's movement. This attitude, according to Sylvia (*The Suffragette Movement*, p. 205) 'gave a convenient handle to opponents, who insisted that the suffrage movement was bourgeois in leadership and opposed to any but a limited vote'.
25.   All quotations in this paragraph from Teresa Billington Greig papers, Box 398, Fawcett Library, London (long letter from Sylvia to Billington Greig, postmark on envelope 17 May 1956).
26.   From 'Britain polling', probably written in 1935, on the occasion of the general election of that year, the first in which women comprised a majority of the electorate, PP no. 166.
27.   Sylvia Pankhurst, 'The chain makers of Cradley Heath', undated, PP no. 27.
28.   Liddington, *Life and Times*.
29.   Sylvia Pankhurst, *The Suffragette Movement*, p. 248.
30.   Ibid., p. 241.
31.   Ibid., p. 250.
32.   Ibid., p. 265.
33.   Quoted in D. Mitchell *Women on the Warpath*, Jonathan Cape, 1966, p. 21.

34. 26 October 1912, George Lansbury collection, vol. 6, British Library of Economic and Political Science, London.
35. Letter dated 17 December 1929, PP no. 11.
36. This paper was owned and financed by the Pethick-Lawrences and hence ceased to be the WSPU organ in 1912 when they were expelled. The WSPU set up a new paper, *The Suffragette*.
37. Sylvia Pankhurst, *The Suffragette Movement*, p. 36.
38. Both Romero in *E. Sylvia Pankhurst* and (surprisingly) Winslow in *Sylvia Pankhurst* attempt to account for Sylvia's remarkable heroism in this regard by presuming that it was motivated by a desire to gain her mother's love and attention. Such psychological ruminations are at best unprovable and at worst subjective distortions.
39. 'The women's movement yesterday and today' undated, but possibly 1943, PP no. 131.
40. Sylvia Pankhurst, *The Suffragette Movement*, p. 252.
41. Quoted in Leslie Parker Hume, *The National Union of Women's Suffrage Societies 1897–1914*, Garland, 1982, p. 51. Fawcett is here referring to the WSPU's decision in 1909 to 'rush the House of Commons'.
42. These figures are obtained from Liddington, *Life and Times*.
43. Parker Hume argues that initially the Labour Party was lukewarm about the scheme because although the Party was officially committed to women's suffrage, members of the parliamentary Party were not united on tactical matters relating to how the party should vote on manhood suffrage.
44. TUC Congress Report, 1913, TUC Library, London.
45. Liddington, *Life and Times*, p. 220.
46. Report of a speech by Sylvia at Kensington Town Hall in an article in the *Manchester Guardian*, 30 May 1912, Gertrude Tuckwell collection. The article reports Sylvia as saying that 'Organised labour had indeed pledged its support and the women were grateful, but they could not bind themselves to any political group'. If this report is accurate it can only indicate that Sylvia was prepared to toe the WSPU line in public at this stage since it is evident that this did not reflect her own position. There are very few published utterances by Sylvia on this matter.
47. *Workers' Dreadnought*, 3 December 1921, article reviewing a biography of Keir Hardie by William Stewart. H. M. Hyndman had died the previous week and Sylvia used

this occasion to compare Hyndman ('the possiblist') to Hardie ('the Marxian'). The latter was eulogised and it is doubtful that his views, edited to reflect her own, were an accurate representation of his position.

Chapter 3

1. Sylvia Pankhurst, *The Suffragette Movement*, p. 416.
2. Ibid., p. 416.
3. Sylvia Pankhurst, 'Autobiographical notes: decisions which have influenced my life', 1937, PP no. 67.
4. By 1916 the organisation (then the Workers' Suffrage Federation) also had 17 branches outside London.
5. Thirty Poplar councillors were imprisoned in 1921, five of them women. Four of these five, Julia Scurr, Minnie Lansbury, Jennie Mackay and Nellie Cressall, were former ELFS members. Nellie was pregnant with her sixth child when she was imprisoned. Her husband, George, was also imprisoned. Nellie became mayor of Poplar in 1943.
6. From the speech made by Nellie Cressall (Councillor Mrs Cressall, as she was then styled), at the Memorial Meeting in honour of Sylvia Pankhurst, Caxton Hall, Westminster, 19 January 1961, Nellie Cressall papers, private family collection.
7. In her autobiography, *From a Victorian to a Modern* (E. Archer, 1927), Dora Montefiore takes issue with Sylvia's version of events in the East End in these early years – namely that the work was started by Annie Kenney (who had been sent by the WSPU to 'rouse London') and Sylvia herself. Sylvia later acknowledged 'these falsehoods' and excused herself on the ground that she was very young at the time 'and entirely under the influence of her mother who wished my [i.e. Montefiore's] name to be suppressed': *From a Victorian*, p. 52
8. *Woman's Dreadnought*, 8 March 1914: article by Sylvia Pankhurst on a brief history of suffrage work in the East End.
9. Sylvia Pankhurst, 'Autobiographical notes', 1937, PP no. 67.
10. Ibid.
11. Winslow, in *Sylvia Pankhurst*, argues that such tactics were necessary to create publicity and thereby recruit more members.

12. Sylvia Pankhurst, *The Suffragette Movement*, p. 505.
13. Ibid.
14. Sylvia Pankhurst, *The Suffragette Movement*, p. 423.
15. She did not change her view of Lansbury's position as time went by. In her long letter to Teresa Billington Greig (Teresa Billington Greig papers) written towards the end of the former's life, Sylvia says of Lansbury: 'to my dismay [he] resigned his seat to fight on the Votes for Women issue. I knew it was premature and that more work should have been done to prepare the constituency first. The local Labour Party officials had not been consulted and were much annoyed.'
16. George Lansbury collection, vol. 6.
17. The Liberal government was forced to introduce such a measure because it depended, as in 1886, on the votes of 80 or so Irish nationalist MPs who held the parliamentary balance between the Liberal and Conservative parties.
18. 19 January 1912. WSPU policy was to oppose Home Rule on the grounds that Edward Carson, who was leading the Ulster 'loyalist' revolt against Irish nationalism, was allegedly in favour of women's suffrage and had said he would introduce it in the event of the formation of a separate Ulster government. This was indeed tortuous logic since the whole purpose of Carson's revolt was to retain the union with England so the notion of Ulster independence was nonsensical.
19. Letter to Lansbury 24(?) November 1912, George Lansbury collection.
20. G. Dangerfield, *The Strange Death of Liberal England*, Perigree, 1980, p. 214.
21. Undated typewritten manuscript, PP no. 133.
22. Christabel to Sylvia, 7 November 1913, PP no. 193.
23. Christabel to Sylvia, 27 November 1913, PP no. 193.
24. Sylvia to Lansbury, 19 November 1913, PP no. 190.
25. Sylvia Pankhurst, *The Suffragette Movement*, p. 501.
26. Ibid., p. 517.
27. Annie Kenney to Sylvia, 25 November 1913, PP no. 189.
28. Sylvia Pankhurst, *The Suffragette Movement*, p. 516.
29. Sylvia reports that Ethel Smyth had said to Mrs Pankhurst that Nora was 'just the class we want', *The Suffragette Movement*, p. 517.
30. Ibid.
31. ELFS minute book, 27 January 1914, PP no. 208.

32. *Woman's Dreadnought*, 8 March 1914.
33. Quoted in Sylvia Pankhurst, *The Suffragette Movement*, p. 519.
34. Ibid.
35. The first issue appeared on 8 March 1914 as a special advance number, initially as a free weekly paper with a guaranteed circulation of 20,000 copies. However by 21 March a cover price of a half-penny was charged.
36. As the *Manchester Guardian* (22 June 1914) commented, 'the women who spoke to Mr. Asquith, and the multitude of other women for whom they spoke, have about as hard lives as any English men or women who can find work at all', Gertrude Tuckwell collection.
37. Ibid.
38. Dangerfield, *The Strange Death*, p. 382. It is unwise to single out a single incident as being responsible for the change in government policy, but Dangerfield is right in drawing attention to it since it 'has not been stressed in suffrage history or in the minds of its survivors' (p. 382) given that the tactics of militant direct action grabbed the headlines.
39. 'The suffragette movement in the East End of London', *The Christian Commonwealth*, 15 July 1914, Gertrude Tuckwell collection.
40. S. Holton *Women's Suffrage and Reform Politics in Britain 1900–1918*, Cambridge University Press, 1986.
41. Ibid., p. 128.
42. Sylvia Pankhurst, *The Suffragette Movement*, p. 594.
43. Quoted in ibid., p. 601.
44. Lloyd George became Prime Minister of a Coalition government in 1916.
45. Sylvia Pankhurst, *The Suffragette Movement*, p. 594.
46. In her *The Life of Emmeline Pankhurst* (Laurie, 1935), Sylvia states 'I did not know until after her death that she … had advocated armed intervention in Russia', p. 166.
47. 'What is the East London Federation of Suffragettes?', *Woman's Dreadnought*, 8 March 1914
48. 'The war's effect on women' by Millicent Garrett Fawcett in *War Illustrated* 6 January 1917, Gertrude Tuckwell collection. This is probably untrue, but it is interesting to note that such an erstwhile doughty fighter for women's rights should want to claim credit for a measure which was so palpably inegalitarian.

49. *Common Cause*, 10 October 1914.
50. Frank Swan, 'Romance in the East End', *Herald*, 2 January 1915.
51. Interview with Sylvia in the *Star*, 28 September 1914, Gertrude Tuckwell collection.
52. *Evening Times*, 5 October 1914, Gertrude Tuckwell collection.
53. Tribute to Sylvia on her death, published in the *Ethiopia Observer*, vol. V, no. 1, 1961.
54. ELFS minute book, 6 August 1914, PP no. 206.
55. In *Sylvia Pankhurst*, Barbara Winslow points out that even doughty activists like Nora Smyth and Jessie Payne supported 'England's cause' initially and that the ELFS lost members and supporters because of Sylvia's well-known pacifism. This situation changed when the full horror of the war became apparent.
56. Ibid.
57. Minute of general members' meetings, 7 July 1915, PP no. 210.
58. Sylvia Pankhurst, 'Autobiographical notes', 1937, PP no. 67.
59. *Woman's Dreadnought*, 29 August 1914.
60. *Woman's Dreadnought*, 3 April 1915.
61. This demand was launched at the 'Women's May Day' organised by the ELFS on 30 May 1915 in Victoria Park, London. Pre-event report in the *Woman's Dreadnought*, 22 May 1915.
62. Known variously as War Emergency National Committee or the War Emergency: Workers' National Committee. Sylvia's papers and the ELFS publications and minutes refer to it as the Labour War Emergency Committee.
63. ELFS minute book, 21 June 1915, PP no. 206.
64. 'James Kier Hardie', *Woman's Dreadnought*, 2 October 1915.
65. Sylvia Pankhurst, *The Home Front*, Mayflower, 1932, Ch. XXIX.
66. *Woman's Dreadnought*, 1 January 1916.
67. A special committee meeting was called to discuss this on 4 July 1915, but no clues are given in the minutes other than bureaucratic and organisational ones, e.g. in the case of Mrs Walker, she had resigned because she could not get on with Mrs Bird; ELFS minute book, 4 July 1915, PP no. 206.
68. *Woman's Dreadnought*, 22 January 1916.

Chapter 4

1. *Workers' Dreadnought*, 2 June 1917.
2. *Workers' Dreadnought*, 28 July 1917.
3. Sassoon was incarcerated in Craiglockhart, an army psychiatric hospital for officers in Edinburgh. His sojourn there is the subject of Pat Barker's *Regeneration* (Penguin, 1991) the first book in the 'factional' trilogy about the First World War by the novelist. Sassoon's declaration, dated July 1917, is reprinted on the first page of *Regeneration*. Interestingly, two of the characters in the second book in the trilogy are non-fictional and had connections with the suffrage movement, namely, Alice Wheeldon and her daughter Hettie. Alice was accused of plotting to kill Lloyd George. Both she and Hettie were members of the WSPU.
4. This is not to detract from the danger in which Sassoon had placed himself. He would have been court-marshalled and shot had not his friend Robert Graves determined to have him placed before an army medical board.
5. WSF minute book, 12 October 1917, PP no. 208.
6. *Workers' Dreadnought*, 3 November 1917.
7. Corio, exiled from his native Italy, lived for many years in London where he wrote for *Avanti* and for British left-wing papers. He met Sylvia in 1917 and became a regular contributor to her paper. Their personal relationship lasted until his death in 1954.
8. 'Marx: de Leon: Lenin', *Workers' Dreadnought*, 15 June 1918.
9. John Reed was the author of the famous eye-witness account of the Russian revolution, *Ten Days that Shook the World* (1919).
10. See, for example, Sylvia's article on 'Germany and the spread of the Peoples' Revolution', *Workers' Dreadnought*, 9 February 1919.
11. For example, a special supplement on India appeared in the *Dreadnought* of 7 September 1918. This contained an in-depth critique, supplied by 'our Indian comrades' of the Montagu Chelmsford report on the governance of India.
12. Barbara Winslow in *Sylvia Pankhurst*, provides details as to how Patricia Lynch managed to get into Dublin – a city closed by the army at the time of the rising.

13. Watson was later exposed as a police spy.
14. WSF Finance Committee minutes, 12 April 1918, PP no. 212.
15. J. T. Murphy's credentials have also been questioned. The late Andrew Rothstein, a contemporary activist and foundation member of the CPGB, in conversation with the author before his death, had raised doubts about the reliability of Murphy claiming that he too was paid by the police. He claimed to able to substantiate this, but in the absence of such evidence, the charge must be laid aside. Suspicions of Murphy probably arose because he rejected Marxism with a vengeance towards the end of his life and, during the 1950s, managed to live with the help of some very wealthy friends including Alan Sainsbury and George Cadbury.
16. Sylvia's contribution to the anti-racist struggle both during and after the war will be dealt with in Chapter 6.
17. This all-party report was issued early in 1917 and became the basis of the 1918 Act.
18. This organisation was established in 1915 and held its first meeting at the *Daily Herald* offices. It appears to have been an attempt to establish a broad-based activist adult suffrage campaigning group linking the left wing of the women's movement with the left wing of the labour movement.
19. WSF minutes, 26 May 1917, PP no. 208.
20. M. Pugh, *Women and the Women's Movement in Britain 1914–1959*, Macmillan, 1992, p. 38. Pugh discusses a variety of possible explanations to account for the inclusion of women in the 1917 Bill. Sylvia's view, strangely, is not one of them.
21. Report of the WSF Annual Conference, *Workers' Dreadnought*, 2 June 1917.
22. WSF minutes, 26 May 1917, PP no. 208.
23. 'Look to the future', *Workers' Dreadnought*, 16 February 1918.
24. Despite its title this was not a feminist party. It was funded by the British Commonwealth Union, backed by the Coalition and by the conservative press.
25. The following year (1919) Lady Astor entered parliament as a Conservative. She was not elected, but took over her husband's Commons seat when he entered the House of Lords.

26.   *Workers' Dreadnought*, 2 November 1918.
27.   *Workers' Dreadnought*, 7 December 1918.
28.   Viz., her article 'Women members of parliament', *Workers' Dreadnought*, 15 December 1923.
29.   Ibid.
30.   Ibid.
31.   This organisation was composed of representatives of the Women's Trade Union League, the Women's Co-operative Guild, the Women's Labour League, the National Federation of Women Workers and the Railway Women's Guild.
32.   WSF council minutes, 12 October 1917, PP no. 208.
33.   WSF statement on parliament and other matters: handwritten manuscript, presumably for Annual Conference, PP no. 218.
34.   'Autobiographical notes', 1937, PP no. 67.
35.   Liddington, *Life and Times*, p. 302.
36.   Quoted in Pugh, *Women and the Women's Movement*, p. 50.
37.   See, for example, Barbara Caine, *English Feminism 1780–1980*, Oxford University Press, 1997.
38.   Eleanor Rathbone, *The Disinherited Family*, Falling Wall Press, 1986 [1924], p. 234.
39.   This legislation was the fulfilment of the government's pre-war promise to the TUC that if trade unions permitted the 'dilution' of labour (i.e. women performing 'men's jobs') during the war, the situation would be 'normalised' when the war ended.
40.   Quoted in Sarah Boston, *Women Workers and the Trade Unions*, Davis-Poynter, 1980, p. 137.
41.   Sylvia Pankhurst, *India and the Earthly Paradise*, Sunshine Publishing House, Bombay, 1926, p. 166.
42.   Ibid.
43.   Ibid., p. 163.
44.   'The last 50 years', undated, PP no. 127.
45.   *Housing and the Workers' Revolution in Capitalist Britain and Bolshevik Russia*, WSF pamphlet, undated (probably 1918), British Library, London.
46.   Ibid., p. 6.
47.   See Christabel Pankhurst, *The Great Scourge*.
48.   Mona Laird was the author of *The Morality of Marriage and Other Essays on the Status and Destiny of Women*, 1897.
49.   'What are the aims of feminism?', undated, PP no. 129.

50. Ibid.
51. Published by Alfred A. Knopf.
52. Letter from Ramsay MacDonald to Sylvia, 19 March 1930, PP no. 10.
53. 'Women's citizenship', undated, approx. 1934, PP no. 131. Emily Wilding Davison was a WSPU militant who, in protesting for the vote, threw herself under the King's horse and was killed at the Derby racecourse in 1913.
54. 'Women's rule in Britain', PP no. 129.

Chapter 5

1. Claude McKay, *A Long Way From Home*, Harvest Books, 1970, p. 77.
2. Letter to the editor of the *Forward*, undated, but probably 1926–27, PP no. 270.
3. Winslow, *Sylvia Pankhurst*, p. 119. Winslow says that this document was brought to her by a ship's physician on the Cunard Line.
4. Rothstein was a Russian resident in Britain and a leading member of the BSP. His son, Andrew, was a foundation member and an important figure for many years in the soon-to-be-established Communist Party of Great Britain.
5. Sylvia's handwritten notes on 'Socialists in Britain', undated, PP no. 79.
6. Handwritten manuscript, 'Setting up the People's Russian Information Bureau', *In the Red Twilight*, an uncompleted and unpublished study of the International Socialist Movement, undated, approx. 1935, PP no. 87.
7. In an editorial (19 March 1921) written presumably by Nora Smyth (Sylvia was in prison) for the seventh anniversary edition, an impressive list of contributors to the paper is recorded, ranging from George Bernard Shaw and the Bruce Glasiers to Willie Gallacher and Harry Pollitt. About a third of these were women and a substantial proportion of the total were non-English.
8. WSF minute book, 26 April 1918, PP no. 209.
9. For some strange reason Winslow (*Sylvia Pankhurst*) regards the talks to unite the two papers as being the beginning of the negotiations for a united communist party. Such negotiations had begun before this between the BSP and other organisations. According to Sylvia's

own account (not verified elsewhere), the BSP made a direct approach to the WSF later, on a separate occasion.

10. 'Towards a communist party', *Workers' Dreadnought*, 21 February 1920.
11. Harry Pollitt, *Serving My Time*, Lawrence and Wishart, 1940.
12. Quoted in John Mahon, *Harry Pollitt: a Biography*, Lawrence and Wishart, 1976.
13. Indeed Gallacher's (and Sylvia's) anti-parliamentary line was quoted and rebutted in full by Lenin in his 'Left-wing communism: an infantile disorder' (in *Lenin: Selected Works*, vol. 3, Progress Publishers, Moscow, 1967) a pamphlet which was written for the opening of the Second Congress of the Communist International and was handed to all delegates. In it Lenin quotes at length from an article written by Gallacher for the *Workers' Dreadnought* (21 February 1920) in which he condemns the 'parliamentary opportunists' in the BSP and the ILP.
14. Pollitt, *Serving My Time*, p. 123.
15. 'Autobiographical notes', 1937, PP no. 78.
16. *Workers' Dreadnought*, 29 September 1919.
17. The criticism of Sylvia continued for several months in the BSP paper *The Call*, starting on 19 February 1920 with an article by Tom Quelch critical of the anti-parliamentary content of the letter rather than the fact of its having been sent. Later, as political differences in the unity talks became sharper, the letter was used as a root and branch attack on Sylvia's individualism.
18. No. 5, 5 September 1919 (Moscow), Marx Memorial Library, London.
19. Ibid. Thus Sylvia did not style herself as 'the leading English Communist' as was asserted by Tom Quelch and Fred Willis of the BSP. Nor was her letter intended for publication – this was Lenin's decision.
20. 22 April 1920.
21. Fred Willis, 'The BSP and parliamentarism', *The Call*, 22 April 1920.
22. 'Left-wing communism: an infantile disorder', *Selected Works* vol. 3, Progress Publishers, Moscow, 1967.
23. Held in London, 31 July and 1 August, published by the CPGB, 1920, Marx Memorial Library, London.
24. Ibid.
25. It was not acceptable to the SLP, however, which split over the issue. Those in favour of continuing the unity

process were expelled and were thereafter known as the Communist Unity Group.
26. Official Report of the Communist Unity Convention of 1920.
27. 'Towards a Communist Party', *Workers' Dreadnought*, 21 February 1920.
28. Ibid.
29. Ibid. It must have been a very small conference since (according to Winslow, in *Sylvia Pankhurst*) it was held in a private flat belonging to Nellie Rathbone, Daisy Lansbury and May O'Callaghan.
30. Letter from A. H. Elsbury of 'the International Socialist Club' to *The Call*, 24 June 1920.
31. Letter to *The Call*, 1 July 1920.
32. H. Pelling, *The British Communist Party: A Historical Profile*, A and C Black, 1958.
33. Ibid.
34. During her time in Italy Sylvia met and was particularly impressed by Bordiga, the leader of the anti-parliamentary faction in the newly formed Italian socialist party.
35. The *Workers' Dreadnought*, 19 July 1920, carried the demand as a banner headline on its front page: 'Do not go to work on Monday July 21st: Join the Triple Alliance of British, French and Italian Workers'.
36. Lenin, 'Message to the First Congress of the Communist Party of Great Britain', in V. I. Lenin, *British Labour and British Imperialism*, Lawrence and Wishart, 1969.
37. Sylvia Pankhurst, 'Soviet Russia as I saw it in 1920: the Congress in the Kremlin', *Workers' Dreadnought*, 16 April 1921.
38. Ibid.
39. Speech, 6 August 1920, at the Second Congress of the Comintern, in *Lenin: Selected Works*, vol. 25, Progress Publishers, Moscow, 1968.
40. Undated, but probably 1920, PP no. 256.
41. The CP (BSTI) was represented in these discussions by its secretary, Edgar T. Whitehead.
42. *The Communist* (issue number unknown).
43. Letter from Sylvia Pankhurst to the *Workers' Dreadnought*, 15 January 1921.
44. Ibid. Sylvia claims that 'Lenin advised this' when she met him in Moscow. This is somewhat unlikely.
45. Elected at the Leeds Conference.

46.   Letter to Sylvia on CP (BSTI) headed paper from Edgar T. Whitehead, PP no. 239.
47.   Letter to the *Workers' Dreadnought*, 15 January 1921.
48.   Article signed by 'A.T.' on 'The editorship of communist papers', *Workers' Dreadnought*, 15 January 1921.
49.   Editorial, *Workers' Dreadnought*, 5 February 1921.
50.   H. M. Hyndman was one of the founders of the BSP's predecessor, the Social Democratic Federation. Hyndman was pro-imperialist and in favour of Britain's entry into the First World War.
51.   17 September 1921.
52.   17 September 1921.
53.   12 November 1921.
54.   Gallacher went on to say that what he regarded as Sylvia's self-engineered expulsion 'had been a tactical error on her part'.
55.   'Autobiographical notes', 1937, PP no. 78.
56.   Ibid.
57.   'Our point of view', *Workers' Dreadnought*, 24 September 1921.
58.   Termed by Sylvia, incorrectly, the Red Trade Union International.
59.   *Workers' Dreadnought*, 8 October 1921.
60.   Ibid.
61.   *Workers' Dreadnought*, 19 June 1920.
62.   Winslow, in *Sylvia Pankhurst*, comes close to suggesting this.
63.   *Workers' Dreadnought*, 20 February 1921.
64.   Ibid., 2 April 1921.
65.   *Workers' Dreadnought*, 7 July 1923.

Chapter 6

1.   A typical example of such racist indoctrination can be found in Fletcher and Kipling's *A History of England*, (Clarendon Press, 1911) a standard text book, in use for many years in elementary schools. Part of the section on the West Indies reads thus:

      The prosperity of the West Indies, once our richest possession, has very largely declined since slavery was abolished in 1833. There is little market for their chief products, and yet a large population, mainly descended from slaves imported in previous centuries, or of mixed black and white races, is lazy, vicious and incapable of any serious improvement, or of work except under compulsion. In such a climate a few bananas will sustain the life of a negro quite sufficiently: why should he work to get more than this? He is quite happy and quite useless and spends any extra money he has upon finery.

2. See her *Women and Socialism*, ILP 1904, ILP collection.
3. For a fuller discussion of this see Richard A. Solway, *Democracy and Degeneration*, University of North Carolina Press, 1990, Chapter 6.
4. Vron Ware, *Beyond the Pale: White Women and Racism*, Verso, 1992, p. 119.
5. Quoted in Garner, *Stepping Stones to Women's Liberty*, p. 50.
6. Sylvia Pankhurst, *The Suffragette Movement*, p. 269.
7. Quoted in V. I. Lenin, *Imperialism, the Highest Stage of Capitalism*, Progress Publishers, Moscow, 1968, p. 74.
8. Sylvia Pankhurst, *India and the Earthly Paradise*, p. 329.
9. *The Foreigner in England – an Examination of the Problem of Alien Immigration*, ILP Tracts for the Times, no. 4, ILP collection.
10. Ibid., p. 3.
11. Ibid., p. 4.
12. Ibid., p. 5.
13. *The Call* was established in 1916. It was the fortnightly (later weekly) journal of the anti-war group within the British Socialist Party. When the pro-war Hyndmanites were defeated and left the party in 1916, *The Call* became the BSP's official journal. Cleansed of the pro-imperialist, pro-war element, the BSP became the main Marxist party in Britain and was to play a key role in the unity talks that resulted in the formation of the Communist Party in 1920 (see Chapter 5). It is for this reason that the article by Quelch and the subsequent debate on race is so significant in that it did not emanate from the older and more incorporated labour tradition.
14. *The Call*, 25 January 1917. Quelch was a regular contributor to the paper. He was the son of the veteran SDF activist, Harry Quelch.
15. *The Call*, 8 February 1917.
16. *The Call*, 13 February 1917.

17. *Herald*, 10 April 1920.
18. *Herald*, 10 April 1920.
19. *Herald*, 12 April 1920.
20. Letter from Norman Ley, *Herald*, 17 April 1920.
21. *Workers' Dreadnought*, 24 April 1920.
22. McKay, *A Long Way*, p. 75.
23. Ibid., pp. 74–5.
24. A claim made by Peter Fryer in his *Staying Power: the History of Black People in Britain*, Pluto Press, 1985.
25. *Workers' Dreadnought*, 31 January 1920. This article is referred to in Wayne Cooper's introduction to *The Passion of Claude McKay*, Schocken Books, New York, 1973, but is mistakenly dated as being published in the *Workers' Dreadnought* of 29 January 1921.
26. Strangely enough neither McKay himself (in *A Long Way*) nor Barbara Winslow (*Sylvia Pankhurst*) who covers the issue, mention this significant article.
27. McKay, *A Long Way*, p. 77. McKay was sharply critical of Sylvia in other respects. He was furious that Sylvia rejected his article about a strike in a sawmill owned by Lansbury on the grounds that she did not want to antagonise him because the paper owed him £20 and that, according to McKay, they were personal friends.
28. *Workers' Dreadnought*, 10 January 1920.
29. *Workers' Dreadnought*, 8 September 1923.
30. Sylvia Pankhurst, *India and the Earthly Paradise*.
31. P. J.Cain and A. G. Hopkins, *British Imperialism: Crisis and Deconstruction*, Longman, 1992, p. 182.
32. Ibid., p. 303.
33. Ibid., p. 327.
34. Quoted in Barbara Caine, *English Feminism 1780–1980*, p. 171.
35. Ibid., p. 170.
36. *In the Red Twilight*, undated, PP no. 146–50. The first part of this did, however, appear in serial form in 1936 in the *NT&EN*.
37. *Workers' Dreadnought*, 4 November 1922.
38. *Workers' Dreadnought*, 9 June 1923.
39. See his *Lectures on Fascism*, Lawrence and Wishart, 1976 – a very influential work which helped to shape the Comintern line.
40. Letter to the editor of the *Forward*, undated, but probably 1926–27, PP no. 270. This is part of a 30-page letter which

goes on to criticize the suppression of left-wing dissent on Soviet Russia but argues that Soviet despotism is quite different and cannot be equated with fascist dictatorship. The file also contains draft(?) notes of her speech which follow the same argument as the letter.

41. Richard Pankhurst, 'Sylvia and the New Times and Ethiopia News', in I. Bullock and R. K. P. Pankhurst, *Sylvia Pankhurst: from Artist to Anti-Fascist*, Macmillan, 1992.
42. Patricia Romero, *E. Sylvia Pankhurst*, p. 210. This is consonant with Romero's 'theory' that throughout her life she had a 'succession of dependencies on men' (p. 287) ranging from her father, to Keir Hardie, to Lenin and finally to the Emperor. She asserts that this 'final dependence, on Haile Selassie, overtook her relationship with Corio' (p. 287).
43. Winslow, *Sylvia Pankhurst*, p. 189.
44. Letter to the author 2 September 1996 and interview 5 September 1996.
45. *NT&EN*, 1 August 1936.
46. Ron Ramdin, *The Making of the Black Working-class in Britain*, Gower, 1987.
47. George Padmore, a Trinidadian, had been the head of the Comintern's Negro Bureau of the Red International of Labour Unions and one of the founders and leaders of the International Trade Union Committee of Negro Workers until it was disbanded in 1933.
48. She explained her views on this in a letter to Stafford Cripps. This letter is in the possession of Richard Pankhurst.
49. Ras Makonnen, *Pan-Africanism From Within*, ed. Kenneth King, Oxford University Press, 1973. Makonnen considered himself to be an Ethiopian and had changed his name from George Griffiths. Together with C. L. R. James and other black exiles in London he had formed the International Friends of Ethiopia.
50. See Robert G. Weisbord, 'British West Indian reaction to the Italian-Ethiopian War: an episode in Pan-Africanism', *Caribbean Studies*, vol. 10, no. 1, 1970.
51. *Barbados Advocate*, 12 November 1935. Quoted in Weisbord, ibid.
52. P. Olisanwuche Esedebe, *Pan Africanism: the Idea and the Movement 1776–1963*, Howard University Press, 1982.

53.   S. K. B. Asante, *Pan-African Protest: West Africa and the Italo-Ethiopian Crisis 1934–1941*, Longman, 1977.
54.   *NT&EN*, 26 September 1936. This was a report of 7th World Conference of the New Education Fellowship.
55.   *NT&EN*, 17 October 1936.
56.   Letter from Sylvia to DuBois, 24 February 1954. *The Correspondence of W. E. B. DuBois*, vol. III, ed. Herbert Aptheker, University of Massachusetts Press, 1978.
57.   Ibid. Letter from DuBois to Sylvia, 31 March 1954.
58.   *NT&EN*, 10 March, 17 March 1956.
59.   See his 'Sylvia and New Times and Ethiopia News'.
60.   *Pan-Africanism from Within*, p. 122.
61.   This, of course, is quite apart from the veneration in which he is held today by countless thousands of Afro-Caribbean Ras Tafarians.
62.   This is notwithstanding the opposition to his rule by the Ethiopian people in later years which resulted in his overthrow in the Ethiopian revolution of 1974.
63.   W. E. B. DuBois' contribution to the 'Words of Appreciation' published in tribute to Sylvia, *Ethiopia Observer*, vol. V, no. 1, 1961.
64.   Richard Pankhurst, *Sylvia Pankhurst: Artist and Crusader*, Paddington Press, 1979, p. 193.
65.   Incorrectly titled the International African Service Board in Romero's book, *E. Sylvia Pankhurst*.
66.   This is a point strongly made by Asante in *Pan-African Protest*, who is critical of historians of Pan-Africanism, e.g. Imanuel Geiss, Esebede and others, for underestimating the influence of Ethiopia on the founding of the IASB and for the general neglect of the link between the Ethiopian issue and the rise of a qualitatively new political and racial consciousness among black people.
67.   *International African Opinion*, Editorial, vol. 1, no. 1, July 1938.
68.   Quoted in Richard Pankhurst, *Sylvia Pankhurst*.
69.   Ibid., p. 207.
70.   Hakim Adi, 'Pan-Africanism in Britain: the Background to the 1945 Manchester Congress', in Hakim Adi and Marika Sherwood (eds) *The 1945 Manchester Pan-African Congress Revisited*, New Beacon Books, 1995.
71.   Richard Pankhurst, 'Sylvia and the *New Times and Ethiopia News*'.
72.   *Ethiopia Observer*, vol. V, no. 1, 1961.

Chapter 7

1. Patricia Romero, *E. Sylvia Pankhurst.*
2. 4 November 1935.
3. In 1924 Sylvia moved to the 'Red Cottage' in Woodford Green, Essex.

Bibliography

Primary sources

Unpublished

Teresa Billington Greig papers, Fawcett Library, London.
Nellie Cressall papers, private family collection.
ILP annual conference reports, Marx Memorial Library, London.
ILP Collection, British Library of Economic and Political Science, London.
George Lansbury Collection, British Library of Economic and Political Science, London.
E. Sylvia Pankhurst papers, 1863–1960, International Institute of Social History, Amsterdam.
Small individual collections, Fawcett Library, London.
Gertrude Tuckwell Collection, TUC Library, University of North London.

Published

Belfort Bax, E., *The Fraud of Feminism* (Grant Richards, 1913).
Billington Greig, T., *The Non-Violent Militant: Selected Writings of Teresa Billington Greig*, ed. C. McPhee and A. Fitzgerald (Routledge and Kegan Paul, 1987).
Dangerfield, G., *The Strange Death of Liberal England* (Perigree, 1980 [1935]).
DuBois, W. E. B., *The Correspondence of W. E. B. DuBois*, 3 volumes, ed. H Aptheker (University of Massachusetts Press, 1978).
Fletcher, S. and Kipling, R., *A History of England* (Clarendon Press, 1904).
Ford, I., *Women and Socialism* (ILP, 1904).
Gallacher, W., *The Rolling of the Thunder* (Lawrence and Wishart, 1926).
——, *Revolt on the Clyde* (Lawrence and Wishart, 1936).

Lenin, V. I., 'Left wing communism: an infantile disorder' in *Lenin: Selected Works*, vol. 3 (Progress Publishers, Moscow, 1967).

———, *Imperialism, the Highest Stage of Capitalism* (Progress Publishers, Moscow, 1968).

———, *British Labour and British Imperialism* (Lawrence and Wishart, 1969).

Makonnen, R., Pan-Africanism from Within, ed. K. King (Oxford University Press, 1973).

McKay, C., *A Long Way From Home* (Harvest Books, 1970).

Mitchell, H., *The Hard Way Up* (Virago, 1977).

Montifiore, D., *From a Victorian to a Modern* (E. Archer 1927).

Pankhurst, C., *Unshackled – the Story of How We Won the Vote* (Hutchinson, 1959).

———, *The Great Scourge and How to End It* (E. Pankhurst, 1913).

Pankhurst, E. S., *The Suffragette* (Sturgis and Walton, 1911).

———, *Housing and the Workers' Revolution* (WSF, 1918).

———, India and the Earthly Paradise (Sunshine Publishing House, Bombay, 1926).

———, *Save the Mothers: A Plea for Measures to Prevent the Annual Loss of about 3000 Child Bearing Mothers and 20,000 Infant lives in England and Wales and a Similar Grievous Wastage in Other Countries* (Alfred A. Knopf, 1930).

———, *The Home Front* (Mayflower Press, 1932).

———, *The Life of Emmeline Pankhurst* (Laurie, 1935).

———, *The Suffragette Movement* (Virago, 1977 [1931]).

Pankhurst, E., *My Own Story* (Virago, 1979).

Pethick-Lawrence, E., *My Part in a Changing World* (Victor Gollancz, 1938).

Pethick-Lawrence, F. W., *Fate Has Been Kind* (Hutchinson, 1959).

Pollitt, H., *Serving My Time* (Lawrence and Wishart, 1940).

Rathbone, E., *The Disinherited Family* (Falling Wall Press, 1986 [1924]).

Snell, H., *The Foreigner in England – an Examination of the Problems of Alien Immigration* (ILP Tracts for the Times, no. 4), undated.

Togliatti, P., *Lectures on Fascism* (Lawrence and Wishart, 1976).

Newspapers, journals and reports

Unless otherwise noted, the following can be found in The British Library's newspaper library at Colindale.

The Call.
Common Cause.
The Communist (Marx Memorial Library, London).
Communist International (Moscow).
Communist Unity Convention Official Report, CPGB, 1920.
Daily Herald (known as the *Herald* between 1912 and 1929).
East End News.
Ethiopia Observer (School of Oriental and African Studies, London).
International African Opinion (School of Oriental and African Studies, London).
Justice.
The Labour Leader.
The Labour Record.
New Times and Ethiopia News.
The Position of Women After the War, Standing Joint Committee of Industrial Women's Organisations, 1917.
The Syndicalist.
A Verbatim Report on December 3rd 1907 – Sex Equality (T. B. Greig) versus Adult Suffrage (M. Bondfield), Women's Freedom League, 1909.
Votes for Women.
Woman's Dreadnought.
Women's Franchise.
Workers' Dreadnought.

Secondary sources

Adi, H. and Sherwood, M., *The 1945 Manchester Pan-African Congress Revisited* (New Beacon Books, 1995).
Asante, S. K. B., *Pan-African Protest: West Africa and the Italo-Ethiopian Crisis 1934–1941* (Longman, 1977).
Barker, P., *Regeneration* (Penguin, 1991).
Boston, S., *Women Workers and the Trade Unions* (Davis-Poynter, 1980).
Branson, N., *Poplarism 1919–1925* (Lawrence and Wishart, 1979).
Bullock, I. and Pankhurst, R. K. P. (eds), *Sylvia Pankhurst: From Artist to Anti-Fascist* (Macmillan, 1992).
Cain, P. J. and Hopkins, A. G., *British Imperialism: Crisis and Deconstruction* (Longman, 1992).

Caine, B., *English Feminism 1780–1980* (Oxford University Press, 1997).

Castle, B., *Sylvia and Christabel Pankhurst* (Penguin, 1987).

Collette, C., *For Labour and For Women* (Manchester University Press, 1989).

Cooper, W., *The Passion of Claude McKay* (Schocken, New York, 1973).

Croucher, R., *We Refuse to Starve in Silence* (Lawrence and Wishart, 1987).

Davis, M., *Comrade or Brother? The History of the British Labour Movement* 1789–1951 (Pluto Press, 1993).

Darlington, R., *The Political Trajectory of J. T. Murphy* (Liverpool University Press, 1998).

Dodd, K., *A Sylvia Pankhurst Reader* (Manchester University Press, 1993).

Frow, R. and E. (eds), *Political Women* (Pluto Press, 1989).

Fryer, P., *Staying Power: The History of Black People in Britain* (Pluto Press, 1985).

Garner, L., *Stepping Stones to Women's Liberty* (Heinemann, 1984).

Geiss, I., *The Pan-African Movement* (Methuen, 1974).

Hannam, J., *Isabella Ford* (Basil Blackwell, 1989).

Harrison, B., *Separate Spheres – the Opposition to Women's Suffrage in Britain* (Croom Helm, 1978).

Holton, S., *Women's Suffrage and Reform Politics in Britain 1900–1918* (Cambridge University Press, 1986).

Kent, S., *Sex and Suffrage in Britain 1860–1914* (Princeton University Press, 1987).

Klugmann, J., *History of the Communist Party of Great Britain, Vol. 1 – 1919–1924* (Lawrence and Wishart, 1968).

Lewenhak, S., *Women and Trade Unions* (Benn, 1977).

Liddington, J., *The Life and Times of a Respectable Rebel: Selina Cooper 1864–1946* (Virago, 1984).

Liddington, J. and Norris, J., *With One Hand Tied Behind Us* (Virago, 1978).

Mahon, J., *Harry Pollitt: A Biography* (Lawrence and Wishart, 1976).

Mitchell, D., *Women on the Warpath* (Jonathan Cape, 1966).

Olisanwuche Esedebe, P., *Pan Africanism: The Idea and the Movement 1776–1963* (Howard University Press, 1982).

Pankhurst, R. K., *Sylvia Pankhurst: Artist and Crusader* (Paddington Press, 1979).

Parker Hume, L., *The National Union of Women's Suffrage Societies* (Garland, 1982).

Pelling, H., *The British Communist Party: A Historical Profile* (A. and C. Black, 1958).

Pugh, M., *Women and the Women's Movement in Britain 1914–1959* (Macmillan, 1992).

Ramdin, R., *The Making of the Black Working Class in Britain* (Gower, 1987).

Ramelson, M., *The Petticoat Rebellion* (Lawrence and Wishart, 1972).

Rendall, J. (ed.), *Equal or Different: Women's Politics 1800–1914* (Basil Blackwell, 1987).

Romero, P., E. *Sylvia Pankhurst: Portrait of a Radical* (Yale University Press, 1987).

Schneer, J., *George Lansbury* (Manchester University Press, 1990).

Smith, H. (ed.), *British Feminism in the Twentieth Century* (Edward Elgar, 1990).

Solway, R. A., *Democracy and Degeneration* (University of North Carolina Press, 1990).

Taylor, B., *Eve and the New Jerusalem* (Virago, 1991).

Ware, V., *Beyond the Pale: White Women and Racism* (Verso, 1992).

Weisbord, R. G., 'British West Indian reaction to the Italian-Ethiopian War: an episode in Pan-Africanism', *Caribbean Studies*, vol. 10, no. 1, 1970.

Winslow, B., *Sylvia Pankhurst: Sexual Politics and Political Activism* (UCL Press, 1996).

Index

Index compiled by Sue Carlton